Leaving A Legacy

A Whole-Person Development Model

Coaches / Leaders Guide

Dr. Ed Gomes

For information on how to download the free power point lessons or contact Ed Gomes, go to www.edgomes.com

Dedication

It is my honor to dedicate this project to those who are and will be involved in shaping the lives of student-athletes in all areas of Whole Person Development. May the life changing principles be used to help student-athletes become the men and women that they were intended to become.

Acknowledgments

It is my pleasure to acknowledge those who have been responsible for the project becoming a reality. First, I want to thank Coach Ken Karcher for introducing me to the Whole Person Development model and for the opportunity to serve as his team chaplain for six years. Secondly, I would like to thank the many coaches, student-athletes and those who have given me their endorsement of the project

Foreword

This special edition of "Leaving a Legacy" has been written by one of this country's premier "life coaches" in the business. Many lives have been changed by the help of Dr. Gomes, who has reached the hearts of people of all ages who want to leave a legacy for the growing people around them. He has designed this manual to promote healthy life decisions for individuals to develop, regardless of the phase of life that person is in. Ed views life as a journey and he believes each person's journey needs a planned course to leave a legacy with success. I have personally used the "Leaving a Legacy" discipleship manual as a guide while working with high school and college students and athletes everywhere. Parents who sit in on the sessions all say the same thing; "we wish we had this program when we were growing up." To be honest, I also wish I had such a tool to draw this information from and influence my own personal journey.

This manual will provide information to help Student-Athletes make the right decisions in life. Learning ahead of time how to respond to the circumstances we face every day will result in a happier and more peaceful life. Zig Ziglar once told me that people are searching for TRUTH and that the best way to find and follow truth is by reading the Scriptures. Dr. Ed Gomes has captured Biblical truth in this "how to" discipleship manual that many people now treasure. Have you ever thought of leaving a legacy in your life? Well, here is your chance to learn how with this unique training tool. The research found within will enable you to practice Godly principals, leading to the most satisfying life that God has planned for you.

Used as a one-on-one guide, teaching to a group or simply reading this for your own personal growth, you will find that "Leaving a Legacy" is life changing. So get ready, the best part of your life STARTS NOW.

Dr. Gomes is one of eleven children raised in New Bedford, Massachusetts. He was offered numerous basketball scholarships, which led him to be a star player on the court at Liberty University. Later, Ed received his Doctorate from Liberty Baptist Theological Seminary and serves as one of the pastors at Thomas Road Baptist Church. This experience, along with his position as Liberty University's Football Team Chaplain, has prompted Dr. Ed Gomes to write these important life skill lessons. Personal experience, blended with his background and Biblical truth, makes the "Leaving a Legacy" book a one-of-a-kind treasure for building lives today. May God bless you as you receive a blessing from this investment in your life

_Rev. Rod E. Gladfelter

MA- Administration
MA- Curriculum and Instruction
Teacher and Football Coach in York, Pennsylvania
Faith based motivational speaker to major college and NFL players.

Introduction

As I considered the thoughts that came to my mind about developing a discipleship manual for coaches and leaders to use for discipling student-athletes, I began to ask myself, What could coaches and leaders pass on to student-athletes that related to the topic of "Leaving a Legacy"?

After pondering that question, I began to put down on paper things that could be passed on to student athletes, and thus "Leaving a Legacy" started to become a reality. The desire from the beginning was to develop biblical and practical insights from God's Word and wisdom from life experiences, which coaches and leaders can use to impact student-athletes.

The insights would be integrated with student athletes through relationships with coaches and leaders, therefore impacting student-athletes who would in turn impact others as they processed what had been passed on to them.

It is my prayer that God will do that very thing as you take your experience and opportunity to influence student-athletes through the "Leaving a Legacy" discipleship manual.

What others are saying about Ed:

It is exciting to see all the years of experience that Ed has dealing with student-athletes being put down on paper and now being shared with others. Ed has a great ability to have incredible insight into many different personalities and assist them in understanding life. Athletics is a wonderful tool to help mold young people and Ed has put together a student-athlete discipleship manual that will lead young people in the right path of life

_Bill Gillespie, Head Strength and Conditioning Coordinator at Liberty University Football

The Leaving a Legacy discipleship manual by Ed Gomes is a great tool FULL of Nuggets that serves as a reminder, refresher and a rebuilder for us all. I have integrated some of the sections into what I am already doing with my one-on-one and small groups. It complements it very well. I highly recommend it

_Johnny Shelton, Former FCA Chaplain at Virginia Tech Football

Dr. Ed Gomes with the inspiration of God and his vast experience as Team Chaplain has put together the most in depth instruction manual for disciple making I have read in a long time. With his attention to spiritual detail, Ed has provided a resource that is long overdue, for the one place where legends are made but more importantly, where "Leaving a Legacy" is so important

_Derrick Moore, FCA Chaplain at Georgia Tech Football

What former players are saying about Ed:

Testimonies from Liberty University football players who have been disciple by Ed Gomes using the "Leaving a Legacy" discipleship manual:

I am in grateful debt to the leadership and intentional relationship that Ed Gomes built with me as a student-athlete at Liberty University. Our weekly meetings were catalytic in my life and sharpened me to become a godlier man, leader, and servant. With relentless persistence, he cared for me, prayed for me, instructed me, opened doors for my life, lead me, and believed in me. He ultimately put the wind in my sails to reproduce the same kind of leaders he is producing; and what better way to pay my debt than leave that same kind of legacy wherever I may go

-Zack Duke Receiver; Luke 2:52 Award recipient and Rock Royer / Mac Rivera Award

The weekly one on one meeting that I had with Dr. Gomes was the highlight of my week. It was something I always looked forward to. Not only was he a mentor to me but he was also a friend. He was always looking out for me and looking out for my best interest. He was honest when I was wrong about something and an encouragement to me in my spiritual walk. I could not ask for a better mentor in my life during my college years. He gave me great advice about relationships, my spiritual walk, and family and trained me how to lead my future wife and family. At the end of every meeting, he made it a point to pray for the team and for me personally. I cannot put into words how much Ed Gomes means to me. I only hope that I can one day have an impact in a man's life like the impact he has had on mine

_Kyle DeArmon   Receiver

It meant accountability. It was good to be able to meet with someone who is spiritual who will help you stay on track as a Christ follower. It was something to help me continue growing as a young man

_Cory Freeman   Defensive Lineman

One-on-one meetings with Ed Gomes were always a unique and special opportunity to receive wisdom and guidance. The ability to bring all the avenues of life from sports, academics, relationships, and life in general, and have an open and honest discussion was truly a blessing. Gomes provided a guiding and loving hand, which helped shape and mold me into the man I am today. I will always be indebted for him pouring into me during our many one-on-one meetings

_Grant Bowdon   Punter

Introduction Lessons

How to Effectively Use the Leaving a Legacy Discipleship Manual

Familiarize yourself with the Leaving A Legacy introduction material

Give special attention to the following lessons

How to understand the Whole Person Development model

How to minister to teammates in the High, Some, No interests

Look at the characteristics of the High, Some, No interests groups

Think through the who, what, when, where, why, and how you will teach the material.

Questions to ask?

Who will I teach?

What will I teach?

When will I teach it?

Where will I teach?

Why will I teach?

How will I teach?

Explain what your expectations will be.

Allow the Holy Spirit to guide you

Teach to change lives

How to Get the Most from Studying the Life Changing Principles (Student-Athletes)

Be teachable

Be on time for appointment
(If you cannot keep the appointment communicate)

Be responsible

Review the topic discussed at least one time after the session

Be flexible (Make the meeting time a priority)

Attempt to share what is being learned with others

Be sure to cross off the number after each topic has been discussed

Look for ways to put into practice what is being learned

How to Use the Topic, Verse, Ice Breaker Question, Principles, Quote and Key Question When Teaching the Life Changing Principles

Remember, each part of the lesson provides a platform to teach spiritual truth.

Don't be afraid to share your ideas or insights that can complement the lesson.

Look for creative ways to illustrate the lesson being taught

Depend on God to use you as you teach the lesson

Remember, it's not just about getting through the lesson, but allowing the Holy Spirit to bring about transformation through the lesson

How to Use the One on One Format for Teaching the Life Changing Principles

Set up the <u>best</u> time and day for the meeting

Remember, just before the lesson begins each person has the chance to ask <u>general</u> questions related to the previous week

Remember, once the lesson is <u>ready</u> to be taught somebody opens the meeting in prayer

Remember, after general questions have been asked, each person has the opportunity to ask one <u>specific</u> question about any area in the life of the other person

Remember, each person has a chance every other week to <u>select</u> the lesson to be discussed

Remember to begin the lesson by looking up the <u>scripture</u> and then introducing the ice breaker question for the lesson

Remember, after the lesson has been covered, prayer <u>requests</u> will be taken and then someone will close in prayer

Don't forget to <u>refer</u> to the purpose, goal and expectation and how the Student-Athlete can get the most out of the lesson

Remember to let God <u>use</u> your style of teaching, illustrations and personality to teach the lesson

How to Use the Team Format for Teaching the Life Changing Principles

Set up the best time and day to teach the lesson

Remember, once the lesson is ready to be taught, somebody opens the meeting in prayer

Remember, once the preliminaries have been talked about, the lesson begins with the topic introduction question

Remember, student-athletes have the opportunity during the lesson to ask questions

Remember, after the lesson has been covered, someone will close in prayer

Remember to let God use your style of teaching, illustrations and personality to teach the lesson

How to Utilize the Purpose, Goal and Expectation for the Life Changing Principles

Understand the Purpose

The purpose for developing the Life Changing Principles is to offer biblical and practical tools for student-athletes and others to use for personal, professional and spiritual development.

Remember the Goal

The goal for developing the Life Changing Principles is for student-athletes and others to experience the life changing power of the gospel and the ability to experience the inward and outward transformation of attitudes and actions.

Know the Expectation

The expectation for developing the Life Changing Principles is to use each lesson as a platform to teach spiritual truth. The lessons provide opportunities to ask questions related to the topic and content being presented during each lesson.

How to Put into Action a Spiritual Game Plan to Impact the Entire Team Through the Life Changing Principles

Determine who will be the spiritual leader to lead each position group spiritually

Identify other spiritual minded teammates in the position group who want to be intentional about their relationship with God and impact teammates

Commit to meet with those spiritual leaders one-on-one or as a group once a week for instruction, encouragement and accountability

Utilize the Life Changing Principles to teach spiritual leaders how to be light and salt to teammates

Continue to encourage them on a regular basis

Trust God to bless your faithfulness

How to Act Properly On a Date

Romans 6:12-13, 13:14, 8:5-9, I Thessalonians 4:1-8

Why is it important to be the right person on a date?

Treat your date like you would want someone to treat your sister or brother on a date

Place yourselves where you can be seen by others

Learn to practice the presence of God

Don't start something physically you cannot finish

Know where you are going ahead of time

Give each other permission to hold each other accountable

Exercise self-discipline

Return to your original destination on time (Communication)

Boundaries surround the life God has given you to maintain and mature, so that you can become the person He created you to be

_Dr. Henry Cloud

How will you put into action what you have learned today?

How to Apply God's Word

Matthew 7:24-27, Luke 11:27-28, James 1:22-24

Why should we put God's Word into action?

Be <u>aware</u> of what the Holy Spirit might be saying through the Word

Properly <u>interpret</u> what you are reading in the Word

Seek <u>guidance</u> from a more mature Christian if you are not sure about what application should be taken from the Word

Be willing to <u>mix</u> faith and obedience with what is revealed from the Word

God gave us His owner's manual, the Bible, to help us avoid breakdowns – morally, ethically, spiritually, and relationally – and to perform at peak performance. His greatest desire is that we develop a wholeness in our lives that allows our walk to match our talk because it is based on a solid belief system

_Bob Reccord

How will you put into action what you have learned today?

How to Apply the Hammer and Chisel Principle

Exodus 3:10, 19-20, 8:19, Luke 15:11-20

Who are some people and circumstances God could be using to shape you?

Remember, it's about responding not reacting

Remember, it's about the who (people) and the what (circumstances) when it comes to responding properly

Remember, it's about asking the right questions about God, self and others

Remember, God can use people and circumstances to bring about salvation, sanctification, or character development

God
People
Circumstances
You and I

God takes us through a spiritual expansion program to enlarge us so we can enjoy greater spiritual growth and manifold blessings. Often, He uses other people as hammers and presses, tempering and shaping the metal of our lives

_Reggie McNeal

How will you put into action what you have learned today?

See App. 1

How to Avoid Making Harmful Decisions

Proverbs 4:14-15, 25-27 12:26, 13:20, 14:16

How can we avoid making harmful choices?

Don't put yourself in a predicament that could get you into trouble

Pay attention to the voices of reason

Be on your guard at all times

Remember, your actions have consequences

Don't be afraid to ask for help if you need it

Remember, you are held to a higher standard

Continually develop habits that lead to good choices

When you associate with winners, your chances of winning go up

_Zig Ziglar

How will you put into action what you have learned today?

How to Avoid Spiritual Complacency

Revelation 2:1-5

How can a person become spiritually complacent?

Know what your spiritual game plan includes for your spiritual development

Be aware of any negative changes in behavior patterns

Allow at least one person the freedom to ask personal accountability questions

Pay attention to things that could lead to spiritual complacency

Seek to develop consistency in your spiritual disciplines

Remember spiritual maturity is not a sprint, it's a marathon

Learn to coach yourself regularly

We must learn to soundproof the heart against the intruding noises of the public world in order to hear what God has to say

_Gordon MacDonald

How will you put into action what you have learned today?

How to Be Salt and Light to Teammates

Matthew 5:13-16, Philippians 2:14-15

How do we reflect God's light to others?

<u>Reflect</u> Christ-likeness through your attitudes and actions

Take <u>responsibility</u> for negative attitudes and actions

Be <u>open</u> to constructive criticism from others

Let your actions <u>speak</u> louder than your words

Give God the <u>praise</u> for what He is doing through you

The more we devote ourselves to emulating the thought and behavioral patterns of Jesus, the more God is able to bless us and use us for His purposes

_Bill Thrall

How will you put into action what you have learned today?

How to Be a Leader On and Off the Field

Joshua 1:6-7, Matthew 5:16

What does it mean to be a leader?

Commit to leading by example

Be open to receiving instruction from others

Be aware of what is taking place around you

Look for practical ways to encourage teammates

Seek to involve others in the leadership process

Let your actions speak louder than your words

Attempt to lead all areas of Whole Person Development

Look for opportunities to demonstrate servant-leadership

A good leader gets people to follow him because they want to, not because he makes them

_Tony Dungy

How will you put into action what you have learned today?

How to Be a Spiritual Leader

Mark 10: 43-44, Acts 6:3-6

What does it mean to be a spiritual leader?

Attempt to lead by example

Incorporate spiritual disciplines in daily life (Word, Prayer)

Learn to coach yourself

Be available for God to use you

Be open to constructive criticism

Seek to practice servant-leadership

Be faithful in the little things

Attempt to live-out biblical character qualities in front of others

A key to effective leadership is our personal, intimate, ongoing, and ever deepening relationship with God

_Dr. Chuck Miller

How will you put into action what you have learned today?

How to be an Example to Teammates

Philippians 3:17, I Timothy 4:11-12

Why is it important to be an example to others?

Remember, it starts with <u>you</u> setting the proper example

Remember, your <u>walk</u> must match your talk

Be responsible for your <u>negative</u> attitudes and actions toward others

Identify everyday <u>situations</u> that help you speak into the lives of teammates through your example

Remember, it's about <u>earning</u> the right to be heard everyday

Leading by example means that you can lead yourself

_Jeff Jansen

How will you put into action what you have learned today?

How to Be Available for God to Use Me to Impact Teammates

Genesis 40:1-19

What does it mean to be available for God to use you?

Be attentive and alert to what is taking place around you

Look for opportunities to be a blessing to teammates

Be mindful that God desires to use you

Make yourself available for God to use you

Remember, each encounter can be a divine appointment

Depend on God for His results

The more we offer ourselves to God's greater purpose, the more we see His hand at work, and consequently the more confident we will become in His plans for us and for the world

_Tom Mullins

How will you put into action what you have learned today?

How to Be Socially Accepted Without Compromising

John 18:15-18, Galatians 2:11-18

Is compromising really worth it in the long run?

Don't forget, compromising causes one to <u>lose</u> credibility, not earn it

Remember, your <u>value</u> is not determined by what others think about you

Keep in mind it's about being in the right <u>position</u> to influence

Ask <u>God</u> for wisdom when being asked to compromise

Attempt to always do the <u>right</u> thing with the proper attitude and humility

Seek <u>advice</u> from another person if you are not sure how to respond

Remember, it's about <u>earning</u> the right to be heard

An appeaser is one who feeds a crocodile - hoping it will eat him last

_Winston Churchill

How will you put into action what you have learned today?

How to Change the Habit of Lying or Cheating

Proverbs 12:19-20, Ephesians 4:25

How does bad behavior set us up for failure?

Remember, behavior can be changed

Remember, being truthful with yourself and others is always best

Remember, it is not just about your reputation, it's about your character

Remember, it will not only benefit you now, but later on in life

Remember, it is not always the easiest thing to do

Remember, it is one good choice at a time
(See lesson number 117 for the step-by-step plan)

Sometimes we don't have enough respect for the power of evil. Often our greatest protection against sin is a wholesome respect for its power

_Barry Black

How will you put into action what you have learned today?

How to Choose the Right Person to Date

I Corinthians 6:39, II Corinthians 6:14-18

What are you looking for in the person you want to date?

Remember, it's about asking the right questions

Is the person a Christian?

What attracts me to the person?

Are spiritual matters a priority to the person?

Does the person attend church on a regular basis?

Is the person accountable to anyone?

Who does the person associate with regularly?

Dating gives people the opportunity to learn about themselves, others, and relationships in a safe context

_Dr. Henry Cloud

How will you put into action what you have learned today?

How to Coach Myself

Psalm 139:23-24, Matt.7:3-5

What are some benefits we receive from correcting ourselves?

Remember, coaching yourself involves a three-fold perspective

1. Looking at life from a divine perspective
2. Looking at life from my perspective
3. Looking at life from another's perspective

Remember, if you don't coach yourself, someone or something else will coach you

Remember, coaching yourself involves honesty and humility during the process

Remember, coaching yourself enhances maturity

Remember, coaching yourself brings great satisfaction

The best measure of a man's honesty isn't his income tax return. It's the zero adjust on his bathroom scale

_Mark Rutland

How will you put into action what you have learned today?

How to Deal with Conflict

Matthew 5:23-26, 18:15-17

Can anything good come from experiencing conflict?

Realize the <u>situation</u> surfaced for a reason

Don't <u>ignore</u> it

Respond to it - don't <u>react</u> to it

Attempt to see the big <u>picture</u> (Communicate with others if needed)

Let it become a <u>teachable</u> moment for everyone involved

Don't <u>jump</u> to conclusions without asking appropriate questions first

Do your <u>best</u> and let God take care of the rest

Every relationship has the potential of becoming the place of transforming encounter with God, and every advance in the spiritual life has its necessary and immediate corollary in the transformation of our relationships with others

_Robert MulHolland

How will you put into action what you have learned today?

How to Deal with Sexual Temptation

Proverbs 3:7-8, I Corinthians 10:13, II Tim. 2:22, James 1:12-16

Why should we avoid sexual temptation?

Maintain a daily time in the Word and prayer

Remember, it's not the first look, but the second look that can begin to set us up for failure

Learn to practice bouncing your eyes immediately

Commit to memorizing and meditating on scripture and character qualities on a regular basis

Coach yourself promptly

Develop a habit of listening to healthy music

Remember, failure to establish good moral patterns leads to a distorted lifestyle

Establish personal accountability with one other person outside your family

Look up the xxxchurch.com website for valuable resources

Seek pastoral or professional assistance if needed

When God loves you enough to give you an internal warning about danger of temptation, listen to the alarm

_Bob Reccord

How will you put into action what you have learned today?

How to Demonstrate Leadership

Luke 9:23, Acts 6:1-7, Philippians 2:3-4

What is one way to demonstrate leadership?

Remember it begins by being an example

Look for things that need to be done and help others to engage in the process as well

Remember leadership is knowing when to stand up, speak up and shut up

Don't forget leadership is both non-verbal and verbal at times

Think of leadership in terms of serving others

Remember leadership is about seeing the big picture
(Attempt to view life from a coach's perspective)

True greatness, true leadership, is found in giving yourself in the service to others, not in coaxing or inducing others to serve you

_J. Oswald Sanders

How will you put into action what you have learned today?

How Determine a Possible Vocation in Life

Psalm 37:3-5, Matthew 6:33, Galatians 2:7-10

If you could have one job in life what would it be?

Remember the process begins with who you know

Remember it's about asking good questions

What is my heart's desire?

Do I have the ability, or can I develop the ability?

Where will I get the training?

Where will I get the opportunity to practice what I have been trained to do?

(Read pages 241-264 in the "Purpose Driven Book" by Rick Warren)

If you're going to fulfill your destiny in life you're going to need some wise friends and advisors to help you see a vision of your future that, perhaps, you can't see yourself

_Bob Beaudin

How will you put into action what you have learned today?

How to Develop and Identify Spiritual Leaders (Grow)

Acts 6:1-7, Philippians 2:19-22

Why should we develop spiritual leaders?

Identify student-athletes who desire to be spiritual leaders

Create a game plan to develop spiritual leaders

Provide practical ways for student-athletes to demonstrate leadership on the team

Establish a way to evaluate the student-athlete's progress

Explain the method to be used to develop spiritual leaders

Keep the "end in mind" idea while developing spiritual leaders (The end goal)

It isn't a structured program that necessarily makes the difference; rather, the difference is made moment by moment by leaders who care – for others

_Tony Dungy

How will you put into action what you have learned today?

How to Develop a Biblical Philosophy of Ministry

Acts 20:24, 21:19, I Corinthians 3:5-15, 4:1-2

What would you consider to be "ministry"?

Be faithful where you have been planted

Remember, it is not just about the what, it's also about the how you do ministry

Don't forget it is not only about ability, it's about availability

Develop a habit of paying attention to what is happening around you

Make yourself available to God and leave the results in His hand

Once captured by God's heart, the leader is positioned to share God's heart with God's people

_Reggie McNeal

How will you put into action what you have learned today?

How to Develop a Daily Game Plan in Life

Psalm 90:12, 119:133, Jeremiah 29:11

Why is it important to have a "daily" game plan in life?

Start your game plan with God's priorities (Word and Prayer)

Be accountable to someone outside your family

Learn to coach yourself

Look for ways to invest in others

Don't forget to develop good life patterns

Evaluate your progress regularly

You were tailor-made, carefully crafted, minutely detailed for a selected divine agenda

_Andy Stanley

How will you put into action what you have learned today?

How to Develop an Attitude of Gratitude

Psalm 119:164, Luke 17:11-19, I Thessalonians 5:16-18

What is one thing you are grateful for?

Learn to count your blessing on a daily basis

Remember, the "testing's and blessing's principle"
(When you see the blessing, expect the testing)
(When you see the testing, look for the blessings)

Take the initiative to see the best in life and in others

Seek the wisdom of another person when having difficulty expressing gratitude

Look for practical ways to express gratitude in verbal and non-verbal ways

Develop a habit of seeing the glass "half full" and not "half empty"

Cultivating an attitude of gratitude provides you with the power to endure life's tests and strengthens you to follow Jesus' example of gratefulness

_Barry Black

How will you put into action what you have learned today?

How to Develop First-Class Dating Standards

Romans 13:13-14, I Thessalonians 4:1-11, I John 2:28

How would define a first class dating standard?

Date only a Christian

The guy should seek permission from parents, guardians or respected adult to begin to officially date (Guidelines in hand)

If denied permission, attempt to ask appropriate questions

Be willing to follow the wishes

Hold each other accountable to follow guidelines if given permission to date

Trust God to guide the process

Dating gives people the opportunity to learn about themselves, others, and relationships in a safe context

_Dr. Henry Cloud

How will you put into action what you have learned today?

How to Develop Champions for Christ

Matthew 5:16, I Corinthians 9:24-27, II Timothy 2:3-7

How would you define a Champion for Christ?

Challenge student-athletes to model Christ-likeness through attitudes and actions

Encourage student-athletes to embrace the full college life experience

Help student-athletes develop a plan of action in all areas of Whole Person Development

Establish accountability with another student-athlete

Provide occasions for student-athletes to demonstrate servant-leadership

Teach student-athletes how to give and respond to constructive criticism from others

Look for opportunities for student-athletes to share publically or privately with others what is being learned

Remember it takes time

Leading like Jesus is a transformational journey

_Ken Blanchard

How will you put into action what you have learned today?

How to Develop Good Character for Everyday Life

Proverbs 10:9, 22:1

Why is it important to develop good character?

Identify the character quality you want to develop (Look at the character quality list)

Develop a practical game plan that you will use to develop the character quality

Involve at least one other person in the game plan

Be honest about setbacks and coach yourself immediately

Look for opportunities to practice the character trait that you are working on

Remember it is a moment by moment process

Share your progress with others

Character is so largely affected by association that we cannot afford to be indifferent as to who or what our friends are

_Unknown

How will you put into action what you have learned today?

How to Develop Winning Habits that Contribute to Success

I Timothy 4:7-8

How do winning habits contribute to success?

Plan ahead

Ask the following questions

Is there anybody I need to communicate with?
Is there anything I need to remember to bring?
Is there any place I need to be?
Is there anything I need to do?
Is there anybody I need to see?

Incorporate spiritual disciplines

Continue developing character

Be aware of possible hindrances

Utilize outside resources

Work at making winning a daily habit

The best way to change the ugly, self-destructive patterns of our lives is to seek to develop good habits that will not merely supplant the bad but will unleash the power of God in our lives

_Mel Lawrenze

How will you put into action what you have learned today?

How to Develop My Relationship with God

Psalm 42:1-2, Luke 10:38-42, John15:4; Philippians 3:10

How can a person develop their relationship with God?

Be intentional about your relationship with God

Make your time with God a high priority of the day

Understand that making adjustments is a normal part of the process

Develop your own spiritual rhythms
(Starting with the Word and prayer)

Be aware of possible distractions

Seek to apply what you are learning

There is no growth in the spiritual life without time spent alone with God. Solitude is essential to deepening the interior life

_Gordon Smith

How will you put into action what you have learned today?

How to Develop Safeguards for Using Social Media

Job 31:1, Psalm 119:37, Acts 8:23, II Corinthians 10:5, Eph. 5:11

Why is important to have social media safe guards?

Remember it's about asking the right questions

Do the words, attitudes, and pictures encourage wholesome living?

Is the life style of the person worth emulating?

Could what I say, send or give the wrong impression to others?

Am I using the social media tool like it was intended to be used?

Do the words or message undermine God or degrade others?

Will it be a positive representation of the team?

Does it reflect Christ-likeness to others?

Could the outcome be questioned by the authority figures you respect?

When I master the urges of immediate gratification stimulated by lust, I am on the road to a new freedom in virtually every area of my life.

_Daniel Henderson

How will you put into action what you have learned today?

How to Discern the Will of God

Mark.3:35, Acts 13:36, Romans 1:9-10, 8:27, 12:2,
Ephesians 6:5-6

Is it possible to know some things about the will of God for our lives?

Remember, it's about making a decision on the basis of information

Remember, it's about asking the following questions

Does God's Word say anything about the decision I am thinking about making?

What are the circumstances telling me?

Have I sought pastoral advice?

Here is the decision I am considering, is there anything you see that I don't see?

Have I sought parental advice?

Here is the decision I am considering, is there anything you see that I don't see?

Have I sought Godly advice from someone I respect?
Here is the decision I am considering, is there anything you see that I don't see?

On the basis of the information that I have gathered, what decision does God want me to make?

When the Word of God, the impulse of the Holy Spirit in my heart, and the outward circumstances are in harmony, then I am convinced that I am acting in accordance with the will of God

_F.B. Meyer

How will you put into action what you have learned today?

How to Disciple another Teammate

Matthew 28:19-20, Acts 14:21-22, 18:23

Why is discipleship important?

Remember it's not about having it all together; it's about being available to help teammates grow spiritually

Understand the reproduction and multiplying principle during the process

Be sure to understand the expectations

Don't underestimate the progression to spiritual maturity

Allow the Holy Spirit to use the time together to do what He wants to do with it

Be faithful and leave the results in God's hand

Disciple making is the overall process of guiding believers to be followers of Jesus

_Chuck Lawless

How will you put into action what you have learned today?

How to Discover Characteristics of a Disciple-Maker

Matthew 28:19-20

How would you describe a disciple-maker?

A disciple-maker is committed to the reproduction process

A disciple-maker continues to cultivate a personal relationship with God

A disciple-maker models Christ-likeness to others

A disciple-maker is engaged in developing other disciples

A disciple-maker reflects a spiritual value system

A disciple-maker looks for others who desire to grow spiritually

A disciple-maker does not have it all together, but desires to grow spiritually

True spirituality includes every aspect of life

_Gordon Smith

How will you put into action what you have learned today?

How to Display Character through My Actions

Proverbs 11:3, 20:7, 28:6, Romans 5:3-4

Why is character important?

Realize that character <u>weaves</u> its way through all areas of life

Be <u>responsible</u> for negative actions and attitudes

Know that character is something that can be <u>developed</u>

Keep in mind it is developed <u>one</u> day at time

Remember, it is a lifelong <u>process</u>

Don't forget to <u>share</u> your progress with others

Character is that internal, overall structure of our self that reveals our long - running patterns of behavior

_Dallas Willard

How will you put into action what you have learned today?

How to Earn the Right to be Heard

Genesis 40:4, Acts 5:33-42, Philippians 2:19-22

What does it mean to earn the right to be heard?

Remember, it is something you must work at daily

Be aware of everyday situations that allow you to earn the right to be heard

Utilize your personality, gifts and abilities to earn the right to be heard

Learn how to ask questions that indicate a genuine interest in teammates

Remember it takes time

Begin the process with people you know

To respect a person is not possible without knowing him; care and responsibility would be blind if they were not guided by knowledge

_Erich Fromm

How will you put into action what you have learned today?

How to Eliminate Excuses

Genesis 3:9-13, Proverbs 26:11

Why is it important to eliminate excuses?

Know what the <u>expectations</u> are

Learn to properly <u>prepare</u> to meet those expectations

Let pass <u>failures</u> become teachable moments

Take full <u>responsibility</u> for failure to meet expectations

Pledge to <u>tell</u> the truth to yourself and to others

Do not <u>dwell</u> on what you did not do, but what you will do

Ninety-nine percent of the failures come from people who have the habit of making excuses

_George Washington Carver

How will you put into action what you have learned today?

How to Encourage Teammates

Acts 20:2, Romans 1:11-12

Who needs encouragement?

Be <u>observant</u> of attitudes and actions of teammates

Notice teammate's <u>doing</u> something positive and compliment them for it

Look for <u>practical</u> ways to demonstrate servant leadership

Recruit other <u>teammates</u> to do the same

Trust <u>God</u> to bless your effort

If you want to maximize the effect of your words, catch people doing things right and immediately praise them

_Bill Perkins

How will you put into action what you have learned today?

How to End a Relationship Correctly

Proverbs 12:18, 15:2, 18:21, 21:23, James 1:5-7

Why should a relationship end correctly?

Remember, everybody processes life differently

Be consistent in the Word, (Psalms) prayer, church attendance and Christian fellowship during the break-up

Let it be a teachable moment for everybody involved

Seek the counsel of a close friend if not sure how to end or process the break-up

Think about taking a time-out with a purpose in mind

Apply the character qualities to the situation

Attempt to end it in person if possible

Seek pastoral or professional counseling if needed

Do not jump back into another relationship right away after the break-up

Friendships provide real-life opportunities to practice love and grace, to receive and to give

_Reggie McNeal

How will you put into action what you have learned today?

How to Find a Good Church at Home and at School

Acts 2:42-47, Hebrews 10:24-25

What is one thing you should look for in a church?

Remember it's about asking the right questions

Does the church use God's Word as its primary source for living out the Christian life?

Is the preaching and teaching ministry of the church Christ centered?

How will the church meet my needs?

Are there opportunities to serve in the local church?

Does the church have a good testimony in the community?

Simple churches are growing and vibrant. Churches with a simple process for reaching and maturing people are expanding the Kingdom

_Thomas Rainer

How will you put into action what you have learned today?

How to Gain Valuable Insight from Others

Proverbs 1:5, 19:20, 22:17

Why is it important to gain wisdom from others?

Identify <u>areas</u> of personal interest

Look for <u>people</u> who model that area of interest

Develop four or five <u>questions</u> to ask

Look for practical <u>ways</u> to implement the valuable insight that was given

Express <u>gratitude</u> for the time and insight that was gleaned from the conversation

Leave the <u>door</u> open for future discussion

Approach every potential connection you make with an open mind and with the thought that this next person(s) may become a life-long friend(s) and someone who can help you grow in new ways you never experienced before

_Robert S. Littell

How will you put into action what you have learned today?

How to Get Involved in a Ministry

Acts 1:17, 25, Ephesians 4:12

Why should every athlete be involved in one ministry?

Look for ways to support your primary place of ministry (Your position group)

Communicate with the person responsible for ministry opportunities where you are planted

Get involved in a ministry where you can have the greatest impact

Be willing to serve to the best of your abilities

Seek to involve others in serving with you

Be faithful to God and others

The more we offer ourselves to God's greater purpose, the more we see His hand at work, and consequently the more confident we will become in His plans for us and for the world

_Tom Mullins

How will you put into action what you have learned today?

How to Get the Most Out of My College Experience

Exodus 18:13-26, Proverbs 19:20

How can your college experience be most memorable?

Don't be afraid to ask for help

Remember you reach your goals with the help of others (Frog on the post principle)

Be aware of resources that are available to you

Always feel free to ask questions (There are no dumb questions)

Share your blessings with others

Pass on to others what you are learning

Time management can be either your wisest companion or your greatest foe

_Stephanie Buda

How will you put into action what you have learned today?

How to Get the Most Out of my Elementary, Jr. and Sr. High School Experience

Proverbs 10; 17, 19:20, 27

Are you making the most out of your high school experience?

Seek the <u>help</u> of others

Remember, you <u>accomplish</u> your goals with help from others

Utilize the <u>resources</u> that are available to you

Always feel free to <u>ask</u> questions (There are no dumb questions)

Let <u>others</u> know about the help you are receiving

While it is wise to learn from experience, it is wiser to learn from the experience of others

_Rick Warren

How will you put into action what you have learned today?

How to Have a Life Changing Time in the God's Word Everyday

Psalm 119:16, 18,103

What are some things that keep us from reading God's Word every day?

Determine your <u>plan</u> What I will do…

Establish the <u>place</u> Where I will do it…

Settle on the <u>time</u> When I will do it…

Decide on the <u>questions</u> What I will get out of it…

(What is one thing I got from what I read today?)

(How can I apply it to my life?)

Seek to apply what you are <u>learning</u> What I will do with it…

Share with <u>others</u> what God is showing you from your time in the Word

What I will share with others…

The Bible was written not to be studied but to change our lives

_Howard Hendricks

How will you put into action what you have learned today?

How to Help a New Believer Grow Spiritually

Acts 18:24-26, I Peter 2:2, II Peter 3:18

Why is it important to help a new believer grow?

Select what you will <u>study</u> together

Be <u>open</u> for something to come up that was not a part of the bible study

Remember, it's not about just <u>completing</u> the lesson; it's about paying attention to what God is doing throughout the lesson

Allow the Holy Spirit to <u>guide</u> the study together

Look for ways to <u>encourage</u> the new believer

Use pass situations to <u>teach</u> valuable lessons about the spiritual life

Attempt to <u>meet</u> weekly

Growth in Christian maturity is a lifelong process

_Paul Pettie

How will you put into action what you have learned today?

How to Identify Positive Qualities in a Role Model

I Corinthians 11:1, Ephesians 5:1

What qualities should we look for in a role model?

One who sets an <u>example</u> for teammates to follow

One who <u>reflects</u> light and salt to teammates

One who <u>cultivates</u> a personal relationship with God

One who <u>makes</u> his / herself available for God to impact teammates

One who is <u>open</u> to constructive criticism from teammates

One who <u>encourages</u> teammates on a regular basis

One who <u>helps</u> others succeed in their journey of life

One who <u>buys</u>-into the program

Leaders lead not by what they say but more in how they conduct themselves

_Jeff Janssen

How will you put into action what you have learned today?

How to Incorporate the Essentials for Spiritual Growth

Hebrews 5:12-14, II Peter 3:18

What are some essential things for physical growth?

Establish a practical plan for reading or studying the Word

Develop a useful plan for praying to God for yourself and others

Attend a local church where you can hear God's Word preached and taught

Demonstrate servant-leadership in a local church or ministry outside the church

Look for one person who can hold you accountable for your plan of action to grow and ask you spiritual minded questions

Learn to listen to the kind of music that will compliment your faith and patterns of spiritual growth

Seek to put into practice what you are learning

Spiritual disciplines are never drudgery as long as we practice them with the goal of godliness in mind

_Donald Whitley

How will you put into action what you have learned today?

How to Keep a Good Conscience

John 8:9, Acts 24:16, I Timothy 1:5

What does it mean to have a good conscience?

Remember, it's about the vertical and horizontal relationships being right

Keep in mind you are responsible for your attitudes and actions

Utilize the "reverse gear" (I was wrong) principle when needed

If possible, use the "reverse gear" principle in person (Phone call or e-mail)

Seek immediately to make things right and leave the results to God

Use the situation to learn valuable lessons about life

The six most important words: "I admit I made a mistake"

_Unknown

How will you put into action what you have learned today?

How to Know How We Should Teach Character

Proverbs 13:2, 20:7

How should we teach character?

By allowing student-athletes to see, character lived out in our daily lives

Through interaction with others

By being real and transparent

Through acknowledging our own shortcomings

By communicating the rewards and consequences of character

Recognizing character as it unfolds in others

Character is the perfection of a disciplined will

_Vince Lombardi

How will you put into action what you have learned today?

How to Know I am a Christian

John 10:27-28, II Corinthians 13:5, I John 5:13

How can you tell if a person is a Christian?

A new understanding of spiritual things

A changed life

A desire to grow

Chastisement by God

An inability to sin and consciously get away with it

Christian life is a journey of the spirit that begins with the gift of forgiveness and life in Christ and progresses through faith and obedience.

_Robert Mulholland

How will you put into action what you have learned today?

How to Know If My Walk is Matching My Talk

Mark 7:1-13, John 18:19-21, Galatians 2:11-18

What does it mean for our walk to match our talk?

Remember it's about asking the right questions

What are <u>others</u> saying about me?

Am I the same <u>person</u> no matter who I am with or where I am?

Is there <u>confirmation</u> from the vertical (God) and horizontal (People) relationships?

Am I <u>taking</u> personal inventory regularly?

Is what I'm <u>reflecting</u> to others consistent with the Word of God?

Am I <u>earning</u> respect or credibility with others?

Image is what people think we are; integrity is what we really are.

_John Maxwell

How will you put into action what you have learned today?

How to Know the Difference between Judging and Discernment

Proverbs 14:15, 15:28, 18:13, 17,

Why is it easy to judge others?

Judging draws conclusions <u>without</u> the facts

Discernment draws conclusions <u>with</u> the facts

Judging <u>shares</u> conclusions with those who are not a part of the solution

Discernment <u>studies</u> important facts related to situation

Judging <u>fails</u> to self-evaluate

Discernment <u>looks</u> for similar experiences that can be shared

Judging may have or may not have <u>overcome</u> the problem

Discernment <u>carefully</u> reviews steps necessary to overcome problem

Don't judge a book by its cover

_Unknown

How will you put into action what you have learned today?

How to Know the Difference between Root and Surface Problems

Luke 6:43-46, Acts 8:22-23, Ephesians 4:31, Hebrews 12:15

What is the difference between a root and surface problem?

A root problem is something that may not be seen by others.

A surface problem is something that may be seen by others

A root problem is the source of the surface problem

A surface problem is the symptom of a deeper problem

A root problem could be one of four root problem areas in a person's life

A surface problem may reflect one of four problem areas in a person's life

(Bitterness / Temporal Value System / Morals / Self Worth)

You can't change the fruit, if you don't change the root

_Patrick Morley

How will you put into action what you have learned today?

How to Know What Character Is

Proverbs 11:3, 14:2

What do you think is a good definition of character?

What you <u>do</u> when no one is looking or what you do when no one is around

When you <u>make</u> decisions based on the needs of others, more than your personal preferences

Doing the <u>right</u> thing

Who <u>you</u> are when times are the hardest or toughest

Right <u>thoughts</u> demonstrated by right actions

Character is <u>what</u> you are in the dark

_Unknown

How will you put into action what you have learned today?

How to Know What We Should Do with God's Word

II Timothy 3:16-17

How can we benefit from God's Word?

Read it

Study it

Obey it

Share it

Preach it

Teach it

Live by it

Meditate on it

Memorize it

The Bible is the starting point for all spiritual disciplines

_Patrick Morley

How will you put into action what you have learned today?

How to Know When We Should Teach Character

Proverbs 27:17, 28:6

When should character be taught?

During <u>times</u> of adversity

When student-athletes are <u>receptive</u> to being taught

In <u>team</u> and position meetings

When <u>teachable</u> moments present themselves

While in <u>practice</u>

During <u>everyday</u> conversations and life situations

Our character will be established as we encounter conflict, adversity, pain and humbling

_Rod Handley

How will you put into action what you have learned today?

How to Know Where We Should Teach Character

Psalm 32:8, Proverbs 19:1

Where should we teach character?

In the home

Through one-on-one relationships with student-athletes

When a student-athlete experiences failure

During times of success or defeat

Through the ups and downs of everyday life

Whenever the opportunity arises

No man can climb out beyond the limitations of his own character

_John Morley

How will you put into action what you have learned today?

How to Know Why We Should Teach Character

Proverbs 10: 9, 28:6

Why should we teach character?

Character is necessary for success

We have a responsibility to teach it

The rewards are worth it

We can't assume it is being taught at home

It helps student-athletes make good decisions

It has long-term benefits

Character is like the foundation of a house it is below the surface

_John Wooden

How will you put into action what you have learned today?

How to Live Out the Elementary, Jr. and Sr. High School and Athletic Team Mission

Colossians.3: 22-24

Do you know the mission of the school?

Attempt to <u>know</u> the mission

Seek to personalize the mission

Look for <u>practical</u> ways to demonstrate the mission through everyday associations with fellow teammates

Share with <u>teammates</u> how the mission is being lived out in your life

Give God the <u>praise</u> for what He continues to do through the mission

Trust lies at the heart of a functioning, cohesive team. Without it, teamwork is all but possible

_Patrick Lencioni

How will you put into action what you have learned today?

How to Live Out the University and Athletic Team Mission

Colossians 3:22-24

Do you know the university mission statement?

Know the university and team mission

Personalize the university and team mission

Look for practical ways to demonstrate the mission through everyday encounters with fellow teammates

Share with teammates how the mission is being lived out in your life

Praise God for what He continues to do

When people come together and set aside their individual needs for the good of the whole, they can accomplish what might have looked impossible on paper

_Patrick Lencioni

How will you put into action what you have learned today?

How to Maintain Purity in a Relationship with the Opposite Sex

Romans 13:13-14, II Timothy 2:20-22

Why is purity important in a relationship?

Commit to building a foundation of trust every day

Don't put yourself in a questionable place or position physically

Establish accountability with one other person outside your family

Put yourself in places where you can be seen by others

Continue to cultivate your relationship with God through spiritual disciplines

Hold each other accountable

Remember, solid relationships require hard work on both sides

Don't forget it requires self-discipline

If you understand what boundaries are and do, they can be one of the most helpful tools in your life to develop love, responsibility, and freedom

_Dr. Henry Cloud

How will you put into action what you have learned today?

How to Make My Position My Primary Ministry

I Corinthians 4:1-2, I Timothy 1:12

Why is it important to make your position group your primary ministry?

Be faithful in your role to the best of your ability

Understand your role in your position group

Look for ways to get to know teammates in your group

Remember, you will be taken out of your comfort zone during the process

Pray with and for teammates in your position group

Work at making your position group a daily priority

If we are serious about ministering to people, we could not have asked for a better place and time in history to be alive

_George Barna

How will you put into action what you have learned today?

How to Memorize God's Word

Joshua1:8, Psalm 119:11, Romans 2:2, Philippians 4:8

How can we benefit from memorizing God's Word?

Decide what you are going to memorize

Determine your plan for memorizing God's Word
(Read 25-20 15-10-5 times a day out loud)

Memorize according to need or interest

Use a card system for memorizing God's Word

Remember the following steps in the process
(Memorize - Mediate - Apply – Review)

God desires that we allow the Holy Spirit to use the truths of scripture to transform our character and guide our life

_Chuck Miller

How will you put into action what you have learned today?

How to Mentor Teammates

Philippians 3:17, II Thessalonians 3:9, II Timothy 2:2

What is one benefit from mentoring others?

Look for teammates who desire to be mentored

Ask those who are being mentored if they are aware of any teammate who desires to be mentored

Discuss expectations with each other

Determine what the format will be during the mentoring process

Seek to reproduce what you are going through with teammates who are being mentored

Share with teammates what God is doing

Don't forget to give God the praise

Mentoring is about building character into the lives of others, modeling and teaching attitudes and behaviors, and creating a constructive legacy to be passed on to future generations

_Tony Dungy

How will you put into action what you have learned today?

How to Minister to Teammates in the High-Interest Group

I Corinthians 2:12-13, 15-16, 3:1

How can we identify a teammate in the High-Interest group?

Commit to <u>lead</u> by example

Pray for and <u>with</u> teammates in the group

Look for ways to <u>encourage</u> each other in the group

Serve teammates through <u>acts</u> of kindness

Maintain good <u>communication</u>

Hold each other <u>accountable</u>

Recruit and encourage others to <u>join</u> the group

True love will find an outlet in service

_Billy Graham

How will you put into action what you have learned today?

See App. 2

How to Minister to Teammates in the No-Interest Group

I Corinthians 2:14, Colossians 4:5, I Thessalonians 4:12

How can we identify a teammate in the No-Interest group?

Identify possible teammates in the group

Pray for teammates in the group

Look for practical ways to develop a friendship with teammates

Ask God for wisdom to ask teammates appropriate questions

Be open to be used by God

Without the gospel we will continue to apply such labels and allow people to remain products of their past

_Dr. Neal Anderson

How will you put into action what you have learned today?

See App. 3

How to Minister to Teammates in the Some-Interest Group

I Corinthians 3:1-2, Hebrews 5:13-14

How can we identify a teammate in the Some-Interest group?

Be aware of teammates in the group

Pray for teammates in the group

Look for ways to get to know teammates in the group

Seek to ask appropriate questions that could promote genuine dialogue

Make yourself available for God to use you

The more we devote ourselves to emulating the thought and behavioral patterns of Jesus, the more God is able to bless us and use us for His purposes

_Bill Thrall

How will you put into action what you have learned today?

See App. 4

How to Offer Constructive Criticism to a Teammate

Proverbs 16:24, 18:21, 25:11-12, 28

What is the best way to give a teammate advice?

Remember, you don't always have to say something to the teammate

Be sure you have the facts if the criticism deals with a problem

Always attempt to speak with teammate in person

Beware of the best time and right heart attitude to communicate

Communicate to the best of your ability and leave the results in God's hand

The true test of character: not just coming under others' influence but acting on the wisdom and truth of their counsel

_Bill Thrall

How will you put into action what you have learned today?

How to Overcome Past Failure

Proverbs 26:11, 28:13, Galatians 6:1

Why does the enemy want us to live in the past?

Be humble because it could be you who failed

Remember, it's not primarily about what was done, but what will be done to change

Take the following steps of action to overcome failure

Past	Present	Future
Steps 1-3	Devil's action plan	
Failure 1 Gen. 3:6	Frustration 2 Gen 3:7	Fear 3 Gen. 3:10
Steps 1-6	God's action plan	
Forgiveness 2 I John 1:9	Forget 3 Phil. 3:13	Faith 4 Rom.1:17
Repent 1 Rev. 2:5	Replace 5 Eph. 4:22-24	Rejoicing 6 Heb.12:10

The best way to change the ugly, self-destructive patterns of our lives is to seek to develop good habits that will not merely supplant the bad but will unleash the power of God in lives

_Mel Lawrenze

How will you put into action what you have learned today?

How to Pass on to Others what I am Learning

John 18:2, II Timothy 2:2

How do we pass on to others what we are learning?

Remember, what is being passed on to you, is being passed on with purpose

Determine how to store what is being passed on

Learn how to put into practice what is being shared with them

Share with others what you are learning

Continue to develop what you are learning

A multiplier is a person who is committed to do the task of reproducing his life in someone else, who in turn will reproduce himself in a third spiritual generation

_Allen Hadidian

How will you put into action what you have learned today?

How to Pray for Teammates

Philippians 1:3-4, James 5:17-18

Who is one teammate you are praying for on the team?

Make an assessment of the prayer needs on the basis of what you see and hear

Determine your plan of action for praying for teammates

Focus on what could happen and not on what isn't happening

Appropriate the eye of faith in your prayer time

Look for daily answers to prayer

Nothing of eternal significance happens apart from prayer

_Dr. Jerry Falwell

How will you put into action what you have learned today?

How to Prepare for Life after College

Proverbs 1:5, 19:20

Why should a person prepare for life after college?

Utilize the resources that are available while in college to determine a possible vocation

Seek to talk with those who are in the field you are preparing to possibly enter

Look for ways to engage in your field of study by volunteering to serve

Take the initiative to gather necessary information to apply for employment after graduation

Try to secure your references or recommendations ahead of time

Do your best and let God take care of the rest

The wise person understands that trying to go it alone is a sure way to run into insurmountable obstacles and costly mistakes

_Bob Beaudin

How will you put into action what you have learned today?

How to Prepare to Be a Godly Husband

Genesis 2:22-24, Matthew 19:4-6

How can you prepare to be a Godly husband?

Be an upright example in the dating and engagement stages of the relationship

Be faithful in developing good, spiritual disciplines during the dating and engagement stages of the relationship

Identify married couples who you would consider to be role models

Utilize outside resources on the subject of marriage

Get connected to a local church and involved in a couples Sunday school or small group

Seek to have an accountability partner outside your family

Remember, it is a lifelong obligation

Don't marry the person you think you can live with; marry only the individual you think you can't live without

_Dr. James C. Dobson

How will you put into action what you have learned today?

How to Prepare to Be a Godly Man

Psalm 4:3, I Timothy 4:7, Titus 2:12

Why is it important to be a godly man?

Be motivated from within to be a godly man

Develop a spiritual plan (Word and prayer) of action that will compliment your inward desire

Establish accountability with one other person

Demonstrate servant-leadership when needed on the team

Consistently evaluate your plan for spiritual growth

Be responsible for attitudes or actions that get in the way of you reflecting who you are

Share with others what God is doing in your life

Remember, it is a lifelong process

Spiritual disciplines are the regular practices men cultivate when they want a closer walk with Christ

_Patrick Morley

How will you put into action what you have learned today?

How to Prepare to Be a Godly Wife

Ephesians 3:22, 5:21, 1 Peter 3:1-5

Why is it important to be a godly wife?

Be certain why you want to get married in the first place (Check your motives)

Cultivate your relationship with God by spending consistent time in the Word and prayer

Learn to honor your husband through submission (Submission doesn't mean we're any "less" significant to God)

Be aware of things that may hinder your relationship

Cultivate a sensitivity for the sacredness of marriage

Never defame the character or name of your husband to others

Always look for ways to compliment him whenever you get the chance (Whether he's with you or not)

A faithful and loving wife is the jewel of a marriage

_Lamar Cole

How will you put into action what you have learned today?

How to Prepare to Be a Godly Woman

I Timothy 2:9-10, 1 Peter 3:5

Why is it important to be a godly woman?

Let your inward qualities compliment your outer qualities

Help other men by properly covering those areas where they can be tempted to look

Remember, what you find important needs to line up with what God finds important

Seek to demonstrate genuineness in everyday relationships

Live a life filled with compassion

Always strive to make your relationship with God a priority

Be harmonious with the Scriptures so that you can counteract every lie from Satan with the truth

Be confident in Christ, knowing life is not about us, but living His life through us

If you understand what boundaries are and do, they can be one of the most helpful tools in your life to deve1op love, responsibility, and freedom

_Dr. Henry Cloud

How will you put into action what you have learned today?

How to Process Life Situations Properly

Genesis 50:20, Roman's 8:28-29

What are some life issues that student-athletes have to deal with?

With God's Word

With God's grace

With God's resource of prayer

With God's people

With God's wisdom

With Biblical character qualities

With God's forgiveness

With God's promises

With God's help

The question isn't, how are you doing, but rather, what are you carrying and how are you processing it

_Ed Gomes

How will you put into action what you have learned today?

How to Properly Prepare for Engagement

Proverbs 18:22, 19:14

Why is it important to prepare for engagement?

Commit to following the <u>process</u> of engagement that will unite each other and each family

Continue to sow <u>seeds</u> of trust in the relationship prior to and during the engagement period

Seek to <u>establish</u> a relationship or accountability with at least one married couple

Continue to add <u>value</u> to your relationship by utilizing outside resources

Try to <u>avoid</u> an engagement for over one year if possible

Continue to <u>cultivate</u> your relationship with God

Hold each other <u>accountable</u> for social and physical behaviors

Trust <u>God</u> to honor your commitment to Him and each other

A good relationship helps us to become more of who God made us to be, not less

_Dr. John Townsend

How will you put into action what you have learned today?

How to Properly Prepare for Marriage

Genesis 2:24, Matt.19:6, Ephesians 5:31-33

Why is important to prepare for marriage?

Continue to build on the fellowship, dating and engagement stages

Invest in resources on the subject of marriage

Establish standards to be followed during the stage prior to marriage

Seek to maintain self-discipline in the relationship

Inquire about pre-marital counseling prior to the wedding date (The earlier the better)

Take at least two on-line self-assessment tests'

Interview other married couples by asking two or three questions about marriage

Continue to build seeds of trust in the relationship

Marriage brings two people together who have a good number of human frailties, and puts them in such close proximity that those frailties will hopefully, in Christ, develop muscle

_Dr. Tim Clinton

How will you put into action what you have learned today?

How to Read the Gauges of Life Correctly

Genesis 37:31-35, 45:25-28, Proverbs 13:12

Why is it important to read your gas gauge correctly?

Remember the gauge surfaced for a reason

Keep in mind the gauge can reveal something about yourself or others

Remember to interpret the gauge correctly by asking the right questions

Seek the advice of others if having difficulty understanding or responding to the gauge

Remember, it's about responding, not reacting to what the gauge is reading

No matter what the circumstances are in your past and no matter what obstacles you face in the future, you can win in the game of life

_Jim Tressel

How will you put into action what you have learned today?

See App. 5

How to Read My Spiritual Key's

Acts 15:36

What are some athletic "keys during the game" an athlete must read properly?

Remember reading your "Spiritual key's" correctly is about asking the right questions

Am I developing consistency in reading the Word?

Am I developing consistency in my prayer life?

Am I developing consistency in attending church?

Am I listening to healthy music?

Am I accountable to one other person?

Am I connected to a small group?

Am I setting a good example for my teammates to follow?

If private world is in order, it will be because I make a daily choice to monitor its state of orderliness

_Gordon MacDonald

How will you put into action what you have learned today?

How to Rebuild Trust after it Has Been Broken

Proverbs 18:19, Matthew 26:69-75

What happens to a relationship when trust is broken?

Be willing, from the heart, to begin a fresh start

Attempt to look at life from the other person's perspective

Remember, it is a day-by-day rebuilding process

Involve others in the process if necessary

Communicate victories regularly

Learn to eliminate excuses

Be willing to apologize and make restitution if necessary

Trust God to God His results

Trust is believing completely in someone or something

_Unknown

How will you put into action what you have learned today?

How to Recognize Healthy Characteristics of a Disciple

John 8:31, 13:35

How would you define a disciple?

A disciple has a personal relationship with God

A disciple is sensitive to spiritual matters

A disciple reflects a life surrended to God

A disciple is interested in helping others grow spiritually

A disciple is teachable and a learner

A disciple is open to servant-leadership

A disciple expresses genuine love to others

A disciple doesn't have it all together

One of the greatest challenges in seeking to lead like Jesus is the intimacy it requires

_Ken Blanchard

How will you put into action what you have learned today?

How to Recognize the Different Stages of Relationships

Psalm 37:5, 118:8, Proverbs 3:5-6, 28:26

Why should we be aware of the different stages of relationships?

Remember what the different stages include

1. Information stage
2. Fellowship/ Friendship stage
3. Permission stage
4. Dating stage
5. Engagement stage
6. Marriage stage

Remember, each stage builds on each other

Remember, each stage provides a different set of questions to entertain

Remember, each stage will reveal things about each other that give conformation or a need for re-evaluation

Remember; seek godly advice while moving through the different stages if needed

Our relationships with others are not only the testing grounds of our spiritual life but also the places where our growth toward wholeness in Christ happens

_Robert MulHolland Jr.

How will you put into action what you have learned today?

How to Reproduce Spiritual Leaders (Multiply)

II Timothy 2:2

Why should we reproduce spiritual leaders?

Look for student-athletes who have an <u>interest</u> in growing spiritually and impacting teammates

Use a practical spiritual <u>assessment</u> tool to recruit potential spiritual leaders

Teach other spiritual leaders to <u>look</u> for potential spiritual leaders

Explain what the <u>expectations</u> will be for student-athletes

(Weekly meeting / love in action projects / outside reading accountability / mentor process / feedback, / etc.)

Develop an <u>action</u> plan that could lead to multiplying spiritual leaders

Leaders who mentor potential leaders multiply their effectiveness

_John Maxwell

How will you put into action what you have learned today?

How to Respond to Constructive Criticism

Proverbs 6:23, 10:17, 13:18, 15:3,
Galatians 2:11-16

Can anything positive come from receiving constructive criticism?

Remember, it surfaced for a reason

Be careful not to react, but rather respond to what surfaced

Don't get hung up with what or how it was said

Try to understand what the person was attempting to say

Learn something from the situation

Let God use what surfaced to help look up (at God) look in (at self) and look out (at others)

The leaders should ask, 'Does the criticism or objection have merit?' The key is to get in front of critics by owning mistakes quickly, thus removing clubs from the hands of those who might want to use the opportunity to beat on the leader

_Reggie McNeal

How will you put into action what you have learned today?

How to Respond to People and Situations with Character

Proverbs 15:28, 18:13, Ephesians 4:29, James 1:19-20

How can we tell if we are responding to life situations with character?

Remember, it's about asking the correct questions

What can I learn through the situation?

What can I learn about myself from the situation?

What character qualities can I apply to the situation?

What needs are You trying to show me in the life of the other person?

What is the best approach to communicate with the person?

We cannot hide the reality of what is true about us, because it comes out in our behavior and gets transferred to all we influence

_Bill Thrall

How will you put into action what you have learned today?

See App. 6

How to Respond to Temptation

I Corinthians 10:13, James 1:12-16, II Peter 2:9

Why should we have a game plan for dealing with temptation?

Expect it before it happens

Recognize it when it happens

Respond to it biblically when it happens

Flee from it when it happens

Give God the praise for not yielding to it when it happens temptation is not sin, but when one yields to it, then it becomes sin

_Unknown

How will you put into action what you have learned today?

How to Select an Accountability Partner

Proverbs 25:12, 27:5, 17

Why is it important to have an accountability partner?

Look for <u>someone</u> you can see yourself following

Identify a person who has a <u>balanced</u> view of life

Select someone you can <u>trust</u>

Be sure to <u>discuss</u> the expectations you will have of each other

Be <u>open</u> to letting the accountability take on its own identity

Let it become a <u>life</u> changing experience

Our desire to be accountable to Him and others should come as a result of desiring to be more like Him

_Rod Handley

How will you put into action what you have learned today?

How to Share My Testimony and Present the Gospel

Mark 5:19, Luke 5:10, Acts 22:1-22, Romans 1:16-17

Why is it difficult to share one's faith with teammates?

Share something about your <u>past</u>
Who I was — Pre-conversion

Share something about your <u>present</u>
Who I became — Conversion

Share something about your <u>future</u>
Who I am becoming — Post-conversion

1. The <u>Problem</u>
2. The <u>Penalty</u>
3. The <u>Provision</u>
4. The <u>Promise</u>
5. The <u>Process</u>

(Am I watering, sowing, planting or reaping)

The more the gospel takes hold of us, the more difficult it becomes to keep quiet about it

_Jim Peterson

How will you put into action what you have learned today?

How to Show Leadership in all Areas of Whole Person Development

Luke 2:52

Why is leadership important?

Academically

Attend every class even when your mind or body doesn't want to be there
Turn in assignments in a timely manner
Encourage teammates to attend class as well
Be on time for class

Athletically

Show up for workouts with the proper mindset
Seek to reach one goal during each practice session
Continue to watch film
Aspire to master your position

Socially

Demonstrate servant-leadership through everyday actions
Look for teammates doing something good and compliment them
Help another teammate succeed
Be a positive representative of your athletic team

Spiritually

Let your attitude and actions be consistent
Apply and read your Bible daily
Attend church on a consistent basis
Make yourself available for God to use you

Leading like Jesus is a transformational journey

_Ken Blanchard

How will you put into action what you have learned today?

How to Start Your Day Off Well

Psalm 90:10-12, Ephesians 5:15

Why is it important to start the day off right?

Start your day off with a God focus

Establish practical goals in all four areas of the Whole-Person Development model

Attempt to be consistent with your spiritual disciplines

Use each day to help others succeed in their journey

Work to eliminate excuses

Seek the help of others when needed

Don't judge each day by the harvest you reap but the seeds that you plant

_Robert Louis Stevenson

How will you put into action what you have learned today?

How to Stay Away from Pornography

II Corinthians 10:3-7, Ephesians 6:10-17, Philippians 4:8

Why should we stay away from pornography?

Remember, failure to stay away from it now sets you up for failure later on in life

Maintain a consistent in the Word and prayer

Develop daily patterns that lead to a zero-tolerance mindset

Utilize software that protects and holds you accountable (Websites: www.xxxchurch.com / www.Pureintimacy.org / www.strategicrenewal.com)

Allow one other person the freedom to ask you accountability questions at any time related to the subject

Continue to renew your mind through scripture memory and biblical character qualities

Trust God for His results

Satan attacks at your weak points. He equally attacks what you think are your strong points

_Bob Reccord

How will you put into action what you have learned today?

How to Study God's Word

Acts 17:11, II Timothy 2:15

What is one benefit we receive from studying the bible?

Choose <u>what</u> you will study

Select the <u>method</u> of your study

Develop a <u>system</u> to record what you have been studying

<u>Share</u> with others what you are studying

<u>Apply</u> what you are studying to everyday life

Bible study is important, because it helps us discern and follow God's plan

_Patrick Morley

How will you put into action what you have learned today?

How to Talk with Someone about Personal Issues

John 4:16-29

Why is it hard to open up to someone about personal issues?

Look for someone you can trust

If you have some doubt about the person, ask someone who may know the person

Think through some of the risks involved

Keep in mind, talking with someone can be like a release valve

Ask the person to keep the conversation confidential
(If possible)

Depend on God to guide you through the process

In order to experience intimate community in the biblical sense, we must learn to reveal ourselves to others

_William Miller

How will you put into action what you have learned today?

How to Think Correctly About God, Self and Others

Matthew 16:5-12, II Corinthians 10:3-6,
Philippians 4:6-8, I Timothy 4:15

Why is it important to think correctly?

Remember, you can't control all the thoughts that enter your mind

Remember, you can properly interpret all the thoughts that enter your mind

Remember, the key to interpreting correctly is asking the right questions about God, self and others

Remember, to ask the wrong question's is to get the wrong answers

Remember, to ask the right question's is to get the right answers

If we can get someone to think correctly, then we can get someone to change their behavior

_Unknown

How will you put into action what you have learned today?

How to Turn Insecurities into Securities

Luke 2:1-18

Why do you think insecurities surface?

Identify the area of insecurity

Realize it has surfaced for a reason

Remember, God wants to use a close friend to help you through it

Appropriate God's grace to begin the process

Develop a plan of action

(Word / Prayer / Memory / Accountability)

Understand it is a moment by moment process of obedience

Be responsible for what you say and how you say it

A mask is only the public proof that an infection is spreading though my body. Inside me, there is a seditious, self-destructive process compelling me to hide what is really true about me. It is time to unmask this dark dynamic that compels me to fashion a mask

_Mel Lawrenz

How will you put into action what you have learned today?

How to Turn Problems into Opportunities

Luke1:5-13, Romans 5:3-4

Can we benefit from experiencing problems?

Remember P.R.O.B.L.E.M.S. are

Predictors: They help mold our future

Reminders: We are not self-sufficient

Opportunities: They pull us out of our rut and cause us to think creatively

Blessings: They open up doors that we typically do not go through

Lessons: Each new challenge will be our teacher

Everywhere: No place or person is excluded from them

Messages: They warn us about potential disaster

Solvable: No problem is without a solution

You don't determine a person's greatness by what they have, but rather, what it takes to discourage him

_Dr. Jerry Falwell

How will you put into action what you have learned today?

How to Understand the Process of Changing Negative Behavior

Ephesians 4:22-24, Colossians 3:1-10

Understand, it begins with you taking responsibility for your attitudes and actions

Keep in mind, it is a day -by-day adventure

Don't forget to involve others in the process

Seek to develop the inner person

Remember to include the character qualities during the process

Incorporate spiritual disciplines

Be aware of the following process

1. Identify the problem (What I did)
2. Design a project (What I will (do)
3. Don't underestimate the process (What it will take)
4. Don't forget the praise (What I have done)

Patterning is focused commitment to making a few habits and character traits the normal, the daily, the consistent

_Mel Lawrenz

How will you put into action what you have learned today?

How to Understand the Realities of College Life as a Student-Athlete

Romans 13:1-5, Colossians 3:23-24

What are some realties about college life?

You will be asked to follow house rules that you may not agree with or like

The sooner you learn to submit with the right heart attitude, the better the experience becomes

You will have less free time

You will be held to a higher standard

Remember, you are a representative of the athletic program and athletic team

Remember, your mind and body will sometime not want to do what it needs to do at times

Remember, your college experience prepares you for later on in life

Love expressed through community still transforms people and creates an attractive and compelling invitation for others to join up

_Reggie McNeal

How will you put into action what you have learned today?

How to Understand Who I am In Christ

I Corinthians 1:2, Ephesians 1:1, 2:19, Colossians 1:12

Why is it important to know who I am in Christ?

It is the key foundation block for life

Remember, becoming a Christian is about a re-birth

Understand the difference between your position and your performance

Understand the biblical evidence that confirms genuine salvation

Be sure to separate salvation from personal struggles

Understand the difference of becoming a member (Salvation) and being a member (Sanctification) of the family of God

The spiritual life is not a matter of trying to do things for Jesus but claiming and resting in what He has already done for us

_Kenneth Boa

How will you put into action what you have learned today?

How to Understand the Whole Person Development Model

Luke 2:52

What does Whole-Person Development mean to you?

Realize that Whole Person Development is the primary focal point of a student - athlete's life while in school

Consider the four tires principle

(Right amount of air pressure in each tire)

Remember, to be aware of the Whole Person Development component goals

(Social, Spiritual, Academic, Athletic)

Don't forget character is a key ingredient in the Whole Person Development model

Remember, the Whole Person Development model reflects all four areas of a student-athlete's life

The major role of teachers is to encourage learners to learn not only spiritual things

_Kenneth Gangel

How will you put into action what you have learned today?

See App. 7-10

How to Understand Why God Uses Circumstances in Our Lives

II Corinthians 12:7-10, Philippians 1:12-18

How does God use people and circumstances to shape us?

Remember, circumstances can become teachable moments

Realize circumstances provide an opportunity to evaluate what is going on around you

Remember, circumstances can be life changing

Consider the blessing and testing principle

(Testing's bring blessings and blessings bring testing's)

Do not over analyze the situation

Don't forget to blend faith and the Word of God

Remember, everybody processes life differently

Trust God through it all

A great story is not just one story but a set of stories. The subplots all contribute a particular element to the development of the major line. None of the mini-stories by themselves yields the whole plot, yet taken together they form the drama

_Reggie McNeal

How will you put into action what you have learned today?

See App.11

How to Understand the Yearly Cycle of a Champion Student-Athlete

Ecclesiastes 3:1-8

What does a Hamster do continually on the roller coaster in his cage?

Remember, <u>each</u> cycle lays the foundation for the following cycle

Remember, it's <u>important</u> to make a statement during each cycle

Understand the significance of each of the following cycles

(The cycle may change depending on the sport)

1. Basic training
2. Coaches stations
3. Spring practice
4. Summer work outs
5. Training camp

In <u>season</u> Conference play, Post-season play, National championship

Preparation plus opportunity equals success

_Unknown

How will you put into action what you have learned today?

See App. 12

How to Use Biblical Principles When Dealing with Questionable Matters

Romans 14:1-6, 14-23, I Corinthians 8:1-13

How would define a biblical principle?

Let the Word of God determine the biblical principles to live by

Do not let people's preferences or experiences be your ultimate authority

Be sure to formulate a question to live by from the biblical principle

Let the love for God and others be the motivation for utilizing the biblical principles

Utilize the biblical character qualities if you're not sure what the Word says

Ask God for wisdom to determine His will before making your final decision

Reason often makes mistakes, but conscience never does

_Josh Billings

How will you put into action what you have learned today?

See App. 13

How to Visualize My Role as the Spiritual Leader in My Position Group

Genesis 40:6-7, Joshua 1:6-7

What does it mean to be the spiritual leader in your position group?

Commit to leading by example in attitude and actions

Seek to identify spiritual minded players in your position group

Begin to pray with and for those who you identified

Pray collectively for other players in your position group on a regular basis

Look for ways to earn the right to be heard from others in the position group (Remembering birthdays and other special events)

Meet with the team Spiritual Life Director at least once a week

Determine, as a group, how to impact the whole team through acts of kindness

Heroes are people who make a distinctly positive impression on your life through words or actions

_William Miller

How will you put into action what you have learned today?

How to Walk in the Spirit While Participating in the Sport

Proverbs 17:28; 14:17; Romans 8:5, 8, 13:14, Galatians 5:16-25; James 1:19-20; I John 1:6-7

What does it mean to enjoy His fellowship during a sporting event?

Begin the sporting <u>event</u> with an awareness of His presence

Have a made-up <u>mind</u> to glorify God through the event

<u>Attempt</u> to demonstrate Christlikeness through the ups and downs of the event

Be <u>responsible</u> for attitudes and actions that don't reflect Christlikeness

Seek to be <u>light</u> and salt through the sporting event

Give Him <u>praise</u> for what He does through you

Being filled with the Holy Spirt is not putting gas in the tank, but rather, putting a driver behind the wheel

_Dr. Sumner Wemp

How will you put into action what you have learned today?

List of Appendices for Coaches / Leaders

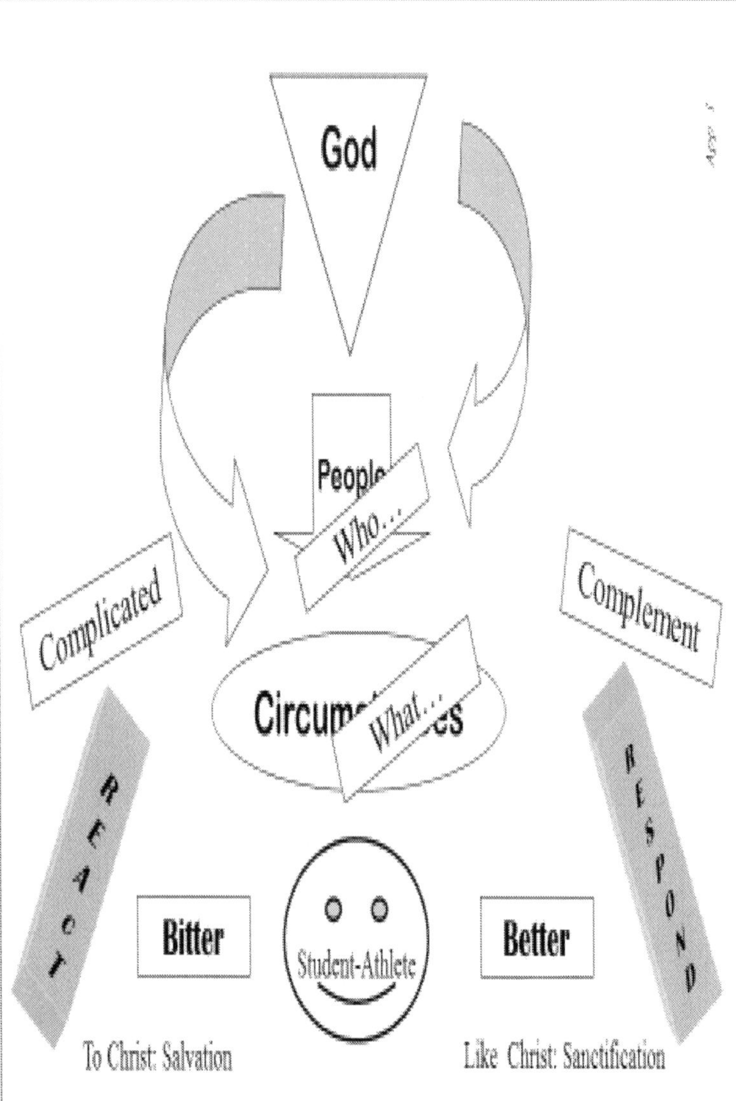
God
People
Who…
Complicated
Complement
Circum… What… …es
REACT
RESPOND
Bitter
Student-Athlete
Better
To Christ: Salvation
Like Christ: Sanctification
Who and What is God attempting to use to speak the student-athlete?

App. 1

First Category of Student-Athletes – High Interest Group

Intentional about Cultivating Their Relationship with God and Impacting Others

Characteristics of Student-Athletes in High-Interest Group

Consistent intake and application of God's Word
Focused prayer time
Attempts to help others grow spiritually
Has an awareness of God in daily life
May attend a local church or on-campus church
Attempts to live out the mission of the school
Inwardly motivated to grow spiritually
Experiences normal struggles in daily walk
Light and Salt to others
Sometimes not the most vocal group player on the team
May assume a spiritual leadership position in another area at school or at local church
A good example for others to follow
Sometimes not the most talented player on the team

Reflections of High-Interest Group to Others

A desire to cultivate relations with God and impact teammates
Individual commitment to Whole-Person Development
Interest in spiritual things
A positive influence on others
Developing an eternal value system
May have been discipled by someone else

Reasons for Being Placed in the High-Interest Group

Has been born again
Is intentional about cultivating relationship with God
Has a desire to develop biblical value system
Has a desire to live out the reality of God in front of others
Has a desire to help others grow
Has an interest in utilizing spiritual disciplines in personal life

App. 2

Second Category of Student-Athletes – Some Interest Group

Could be a new Christian or someone who is saved
but life is still all about self

Characteristics of Student-Athletes in Some-Interest Group

Spiritual Disciplines not a top priority
Temporal things have a tendency to supersede spiritual things
Lives life with a "take it or leave it" approach to spiritual disciplines
Certain events at certain times may trigger a spiritual interest
No consistent plan for spiritual growth
A hit or miss approach to spiritual things
Worldly things overshadow spiritual things in life
Fear of what others may think

Reflections of Some-Interest Group to Others

Minimal interest in spiritual things / Spiritual infancy
Spiritual values are not a priority in daily life
No enthusiasm for spiritual things
Little influence spiritually on others
May have never been discipled by someone else

Reasons for being placed in the Some-Interest Group

Lack of spiritual consecration
Temporary value system
Past failure
Possible personal defeat in daily life
Possible wrong thought patterns about God, self and others

App. 3

Third Category of Student-Athletes – No Interest Group

Maybe interested in spiritual things, but has not given a clear cut testimony of salvation

Characteristics of Student-Athletes in No-Interest Group

Never been born again
No interest in spiritual things
No interest in attending the local church
Over emphasis on self
No conscious awareness of God in the daily things of life
Spiritual disciplines are more academic than life-changing

Reflections of No-Interest Group to Others

Never born again
No interest in spiritual things
No spiritual life
No spiritual influence on others

Reasons for being placed in the No-Interest Group

Never born again
No outward evidence of genuine conversation

App. 4

Gauges to Read Regularly and Honestly

Low -- High

Vocational
Physical
Emotional
Physiological
Social
Mental
Relational
Personal
Family
Self-Worth
Ministry
Professional
Spiritual
Moral
Academic
Athletic
Financial

What is the Gauge telling me?

App. 5

Character Qualities

Alertness
Being aware of the events taking place around me so that I can have the right responses to them

Attentiveness
Showing the worth of a person by giving undivided attention to their words and emotions

Obedience
Fulfilling instructions so that the one I am serving will be fully satisfied and pleased

Contentment
Realizing that God has provided everything, I need for my present happiness

Orderliness
Learning to organize and care for personal possessions

Reverence
Learning to give honor where honor is due and to respect the possessions and property of others

Forgiveness
Clearing the record of those who have wronged me and not holding their past offenses against them

Gratefulness
Making known in what ways He has benefited my life

Faith
Developing an unshakable confidence in God and acting upon it

Truthfulness
Earning future trust by accurately reporting past facts

Security
Structuring my life around what is eternal and cannot be destroyed or taken away

Meekness
Learning to live with power under control

Cautiousness
Seeing future consequences of present actions

Patience
Accepting a difficult situation without demanding a deadline to remove it

Dependability
Fulfilling what I consented to do even if it means unexpected sacrifice

Determination
Purposing to accomplish goals in time regardless of the opposition

Punctuality
Showing respect for other people and the limited time that they have

Discernment
The ability to understand why things happen to me and others

Loyalty
Using difficult times to demonstrate my commitment to others or what is right

Compassion
Investing whatever is necessary to heal the hurts of others by the willingness to bear their pain

Thriftiness
Not letting myself or others spend that which is not necessary

Responsibility
Knowing and doing what is expected from me

Virtue
Learning to build personal moral standards which will cause others to desire a more moral life

Tolerance
Learning to accept others as valuable individuals regardless of their maturity

Fairness
Looking at a decision from the viewpoint of each person involved

Joyfulness
Learning how to lift the spirits and to be pleasant regardless of the outside circumstances

Wisdom
Learning to see and respond to life from another's perspective, the application of knowledge

Self-Control
Bringing my thoughts, words, actions, and attitudes into constant obedience in order to benefit others

Discretion
The ability to avoid words, actions and attitudes, which could result in undesirable consequences

Diligence
Visualizing each task as a special assignment and using all my energies to accomplish it

Endurance
The inward strength to withstand stress to manage what occurs in my life

Deference
Limiting my freedom to speak and act in order not to offend the tastes of others

Sincerity
Eagerness to do what is right without ulterior motives

Generosity
Realizing that all I have belongs to God and freely giving of these to benefit others

Humility
Seeing the contrast between what is perfect and my inability to achieve it

Enthusiasm
Learning what actions and attitudes please others and becoming excited about doing them

Initiative
Recognizing and doing what needs to be done before I am asked to do it

Love
Learning to serve the basic needs of others without motive or personal reward

Creativity
Applying wisdom and practical insights to a need or task

Decisiveness
Learning to finalize difficult decisions on the basis of what is right

Sensitivity
Knowing what words and actions will benefit others

Thoroughness
Realizing that each of our tasks will be reviewed

Resourcefulness
Wise use of that which others would normally overlook or discard

Flexibility
Learning how to cheerfully change plans when unexpected conditions require it

Availability
Making my own schedule and priorities secondary to the wishes of those I am serving

Hospitality
Cheerfully sharing food, shelter and my life with those whom I come in contact

Gentleness
Learning to respond to needs with kindness, personal care, and love

Boldness
Demonstrating the confidence that doing what is right will bring ultimate victory regardless of present opposition

Persuasiveness
Using words which cause the listener's spirit to confirm that he is hearing truth

Courage
Fulfilling my responsibilities in spite of being afraid

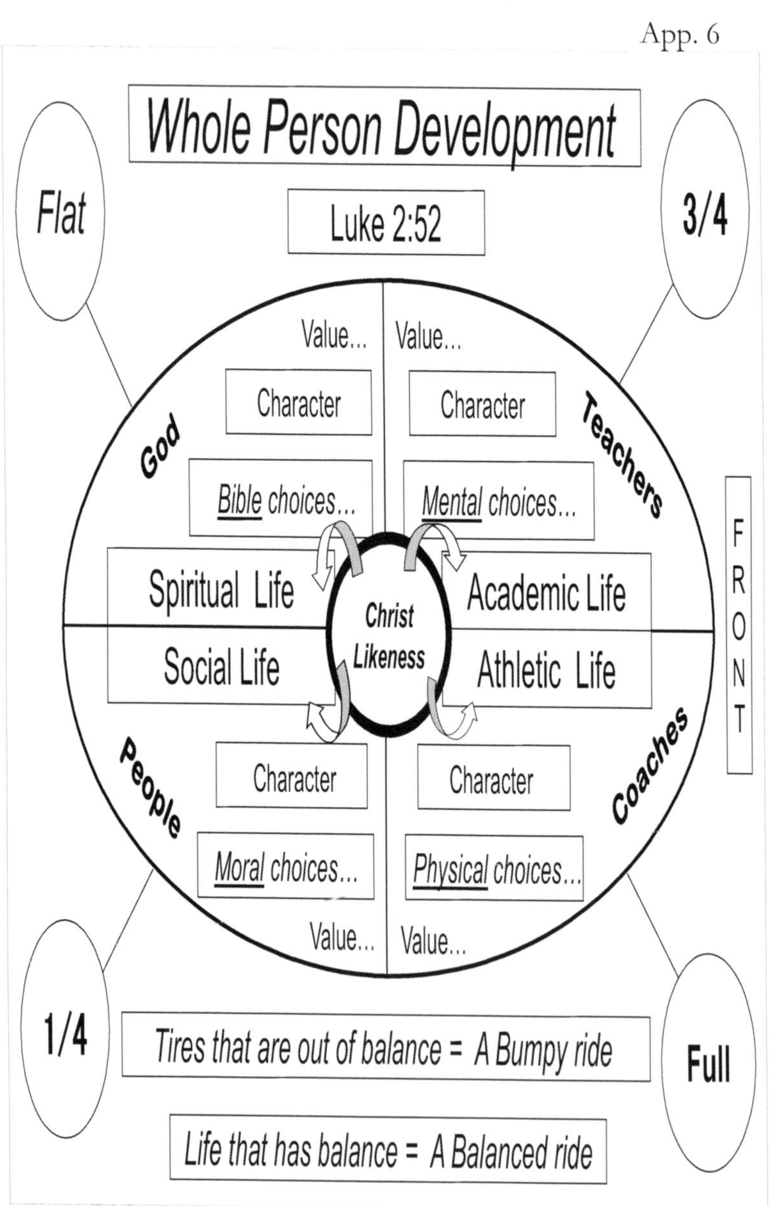
Whole Person Development
Luke 2:52
Flat
3/4
1/4
Full
Value...
Value...
Character
Character
God
Teachers
Bible choices...
Mental choices...
Spiritual Life
Academic Life
Christ Likeness
Social Life
Athletic Life
FRONT
People
Coaches
Character
Character
Moral choices...
Physical choices...
Value...
Value...
Tires that are out of balance = A Bumpy ride
Life that has balance = A Balanced ride

App. 7

Whole-Person Development Components
Luke 2:52

Athletically

To prepare physically and mentally to compete in competition

Academically

To acquire an education for life after athletics

Socially

To appropriate positive interaction with fellow students, faculty, and community

Spiritually

To foster growth through spiritual and biblical character development

App. 8

Whole Person Development Questions for Coaches to ask Student-Athletes

Questions related to Athletic Life

Are you making progress in the weight room?

Who do you hold accountable in the weight room?

Are you eating properly?

What are you doing extra to improve your game?

Do you have a game plan to meet your athletic goals?

Are your goals realistic?

What specific position skills are you working on?

Are you drinking plenty of fluids?

What are your plans for the summer?

What are your physical performance goals?

Are you getting the proper treatment?

Have you shared your goals with another teammate?

How much time do you spend studying the playbook?

Have you talked to a coach lately?

Are you watching enough film?

What Character qualities apply area?

Questions related to Academic Life

Are you attending all your classes?

Are you completing your homework?

Are you using your time wisely?

Is anybody holding you accountable?

Have you talked with your Advisor?

Are you showing up to class on time?

Do you know your teachers?

Are you sitting in the right seat?

How are your grades?

Do you need tutoring in any area?

When do you plan to graduate?

Is your room clean or messy?

Are you utilizing your resources?

Are you thinking correctly about life?

What Character qualities apply to this area?

Questions related to Social Life

Do you need to talk to anybody?

Do you have a girl friend?

How long have you been dating?

Do you have a set of practical standards for dating?

Are you aware of a self-report?

Are setting a good example for others to follow?

Who are the significant people in your life?

How do you get to meet other people?

How do you determine who you associate with?

Who do you talk with when you have a problem?

Have you shared your dating standards with any adult?

Who is holding you accountable socially?

Are you putting yourself in compromising situations?

Are you making friends on campus?

Is there a habit getting you down?

What Character qualities apply to this area?

Questions related to Spiritual Life

What does it mean to be born again?

Do you attend church anywhere?

What is your religious background?

Is prayer a normal part of your life?

How is your spiritual journey?

Who are you helping spiritually?

Do you ever doubt your salvation?

Do you know the school's mission statement?

Are you accountable spiritually?

What is your spiritual game plan?

What are some guidelines for making wise decisions?

How do you determine your identity?

What is your Christian service?

Is anybody helping you spiritually?

How are you encouraging others?

Who do you respect spiritually?

What Character qualities apply to this area?

App. 9

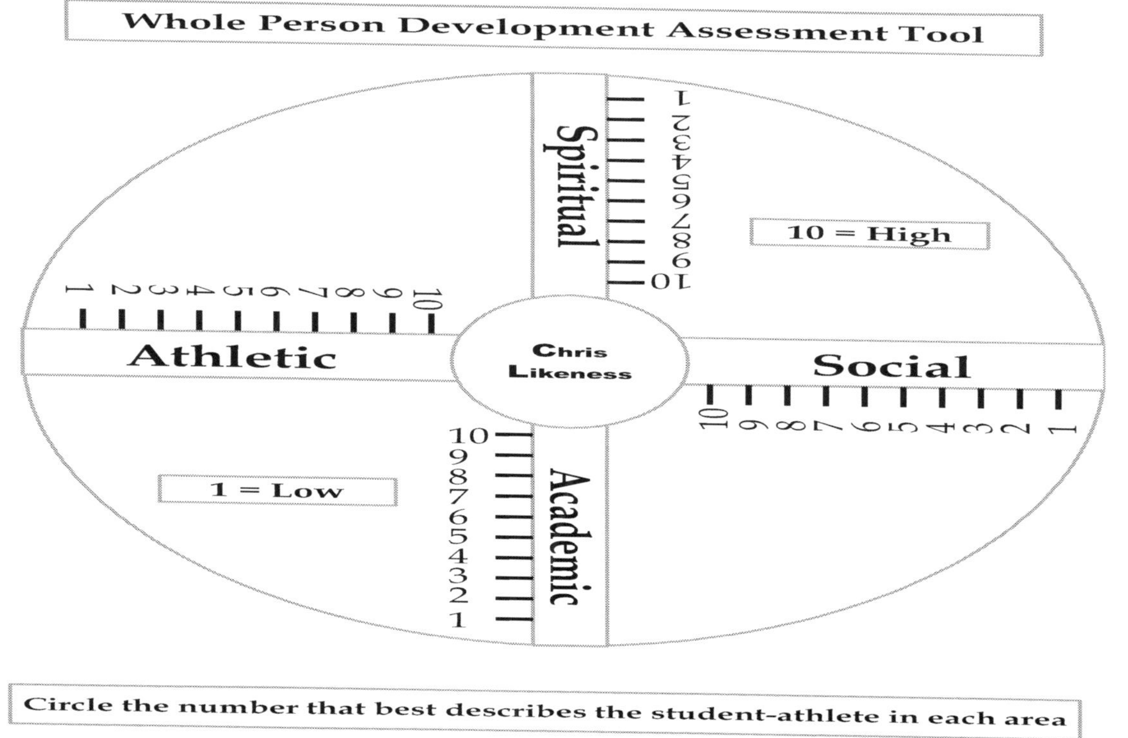
Whole Person Development Assessment Tool
Spiritual
10 = High
Athletic
Chris
Likeness
Social
Academic
1 = Low
Circle the number that best describes the student-athlete in each area

App. 10

Coaches
Station
Spring
Practice
Basic Training
Summer
Workouts
Cycle of
Student
Athlete
Christmas Break
Training Camp
In-Season
Conference Play
Post –Season Play
National Championship

App. 11

Why God Uses Circumstances

The **circumstances** have to do with what He is using

The **people** have to do with who He is using

To lead a person to Christ
Increase one's faith
Reveal an area of disobedience
Discipline a believer
Re-establish positive patterns of life
Reveal insecurities
Build character
Confirm God's love
Look at life from another point of view
Reveal a blind spot
Reveal needs in others
Reveal a need to seek professional assistance
Confirm God's will
Preparation for the future
Make restitution
Reveal an area in life that needs attention
Re-evaluate a decision to be made
Develop humility
Reveal an unfinished area
Evaluate thinking patterns
Restore a broken relationship
Test one's faith
Build a life message
Make a past wrong, right
Help make wise choices
Evaluate motives

Attach new meaning to people, circumstances and life
Prevent something negative from happening
To confirm a need for accountability
To show me something about me

App. 12

Biblical Principles for Dealing with Questionable Matters

The Inward Look:

Relates to looking at life from my viewpoint

Do I have to disobey any known truth?
James 4:17

Is it harmful to the body?
1 Cor. 3:16-17, 19-20

Do I have doubt?
Rom. 14:5, 23, Col.3:15

Could it cause me to go back to my old ways?
Eph. 4:22-24; Col. 3:5-10

Does it produce guilt?
Gen.2:25, 3:7-11, Rom. 2:14-16

Will it distract me from my devotion to the Lord?
I Cor.7:35

Will it hinder my spiritual growth?
Eph. 4:15, I Pet. 2:2; II Pet. 3:18

Do I have to neglect any church responsibilities?
Acts 2:42, Heb.10:25

The Outward Look:
Relates to looking at life from other viewpoints

Will it be offensive?
I Cor. 8:3, 10:32, II Cor. 6:3

Does it set a good example for others?
I Cor. 11:1, Eph. 5:1-2, I Tim. 4:12, I Pet.3:16-17

Is it contrary to the wishes of those in authority?
Eph. 6:1, Rom. 13:1-7, Heb. 13:17

Could I cause a weaker Christian to stumble?
Rom. 14, I Cor. 8:9

Does it identify with the world?
Rom. 12:1-2, I John 2:15, 4:4-6

Will the gospel be hindered in anyway?
I Cor. 9:12, 19-23, 10:23, I Pet. 3:15

Does it edify?
Rom. 14:19, I Cor. 10:23, II Cor. 10::23, 12:19, I Thess. 5:11

Can my good be spoken evil of?
Rom. 14:16, I Thess. 5:22

The Upward Look:

Relates to looking at life from God's viewpoint

Does it glorify God?
Rom. 15:6, I Cor. 6:20, 10:31, Col. 3:17

If Christ returned at that moment, would He be ashamed of me?
I Cor. 1:8, Phil. 2:15, II Pet. 3:14, 1 John 2:28

Can I offer thanks to God afterward?
Eph. 5:3-13, Gal. 5:13, 1 Thess. 4:1-8, Col. 3:5

What others are saying about Ed:

It is exciting to see all the years of experience that Ed has dealing with student-athletes being put down on paper and now being shared with others. Ed has a great ability to have incredible insight into many different personalities and assist them in understanding life. Athletics is a wonderful tool to help mold young people and Ed has put together a student-athlete discipleship manual that will lead young people in the right path of life

_Bill Gillespie, Head Strength and Conditioning Coordinator at Liberty University Football

The Leaving a Legacy discipleship manual by Ed Gomes is a great tool FULL of Nuggets that serves as a reminder, refresher and a rebuilder for us all. I have integrated some of the sections into what I am already doing with my one-on-one and small groups. It complements it very well. I highly recommend it

_Johnny Shelton, Former FCA Chaplain at Virginia Tech Football

Dr. Ed Gomes with the inspiration of God and his vast experience as Team Chaplain has put together the most in depth instruction manual for disciple making I have read in a long time. With his attention to spiritual detail, Ed has provided a resource that is long overdue, for the one place where legends are made but more importantly, where Leaving a Legacy is so important

_Derrick Moore, FCA Chaplain at Georgia Tech Football

Leaving a Legacy is an invaluable tool for sports ministry professionals today in the college mission fields of America

_George L. Morris, FCA Chaplain at University of Virginia Football

One of the most important things I feel like I can do with our athletes is help them study, understand, and live by the Word of God. Through "Leaving a Legacy", Ed Gomes gives simple and practical advice to help them do that! I'm thankful he has provided such a simple and clear tool for student athletes to know and apply powerful truths from the Word of God

_Wes Yeary, Former Athletics Chaplain at Baylor University Football

What former players are saying about Ed:

Testimonies from Liberty University football players who have been discipled by Ed Gomes using the "Leaving a Legacy" discipleship manual:

I am in grateful debt to the leadership and intentional relationship that Ed Gomes built with me as a student-athlete at Liberty University. Our weekly meetings were catalytic in my life and sharpened me to become a more godly man, leader, and servant. With relentless persistence he cared for me, prayed for me, instructed me, opened doors for my life, lead me, and believed in me. He ultimately put the wind in my sails to reproduce the same kind of leaders he is producing; and what better way to pay my debt than leave that same kind of legacy wherever I may go."

_Zack Duke Receiver; Luke 2:52 Award recipient and Rock Royer / Mac Rivera Award

One-on-one meetings with Ed Gomes were always a unique and special opportunity to receive wisdom and guidance. The ability to bring all the avenues of life from sports, academics, relationships, and life in general, and have an open and honest discussion was truly a blessing. Gomes provided a guiding and loving hand which helped shape and mold me into the man I am today. I will always be indebted for him pouring into me during our many many one-on-one meeting

_Grant Bowdon Punter:

The weekly one on one meeting that I had with Dr. Gomes was the highlight of my week. It was something I always looked forward to. Not only was he a mentor to me but he was also a friend. He was always looking out for me and looking out for my best interest. He was honest when I was wrong about something and an encouragement to me in my spiritual walk. I could not ask for a better mentor in my life during my college years. He is a prayer warrior and I knew he was praying for me every day. He gave me great advice about relationships, my spiritual walk, and family and trained me how to lead my future wife and family. Not only was the meeting once a week but it carried over into my everyday life. He would continue to ask me how I was doing, tell me he was praying for me and even make sure I was doing well in class. I can say I could honestly feel the love that Ed Gomes had for me and the rest of the players. At the end of every meeting he made it a point to pray for the team and for me personally. I cannot put into words how much Ed Gomes means to me. He was and still is a man I can go to for anything. I only hope that I can one day have an impact in a man's life like the impact he has had on mine. I love you, thank you for everything you have done for me

_Kyle DeArmon   Receiver

To be honest, I have looked forward to just about every meeting with Ed Gomes since we started. When we meet, I just feel like I'm in the right place and God definitely wants me there. I'm able to just talk as a friend with Ed Gomes while gaining wisdom. His words are extremely encouraging and his way of putting things really allows you to take it all in

_Leo Cardenas   Running back

The weekly meeting has changed my life from the very start as a freshman seeking to find my role on the football field and discipline in the classroom to being a senior and leaving a legacy for the younger players. It has helped me to realize the big picture in life and to learn that it is not about me but it is about the glorification of Jesus Christ who died for all. It has meant a lot to me and I pray that others take part in this wonderful process of becoming a better person and having a better relationship with Christ

_Aaron Brown Offensive Lineman

The weekly one on one meeting with Ed Gomes was a blessing to my collegiate career. The fellowship and building of a Christ centered relationship played an important role in getting me through low and highs that occurred on a daily basis. The weekly meetings were a blessing during my time college career

_Matt Bevins All-American Kicker

The meetings have really been a life changer for me on helping me prepare for life as a man and become more of a man of Christ. And I have been coming out of the meetings stronger and knowing that I'm blessed

_Malcolm Boyd Offensive Lineman

The meetings that we have over the past three years have made me the man that I am today

_Aaron Lundy Offensive lineman, Captain

Meeting with Ed Gomes has meant the world to me. It has given me an opportunity to gain incredible wisdom and insight from a great source. He has poured into me in a very stressful time, and for that I am forever grateful

_Brandon Robinson Defensive Back, Captain

Meeting with Ed Gomes has been a consistent source of joy and encouragement in my life. Gomes has both challenged me when I needed spurring along, while encouraging me in the midst of a long year-cycle that student athletes go through. I have benefited greatly from Ed Gomes being an accountability partner and spiritual mentor in my life

_Brandon Apon Tight End

I truly have enjoyed meeting every week because whenever we met we both ALWAYS got blessed. It was something that I looked forward to whenever we got the chance to do so. You are definitely someone I look up to have my back and someone I can always come to. I truly appreciate you in all that you do

_Kevin Fogg Defensive Back / All-American Punt and Kick Returner

It meant accountability. It was good to be able to meet with someone who is spiritual who will help you stay on track as a Christ follower. It was something to help me continue growing as a young man

_Cory Freeman Defensive Lineman

The once a week meeting, is probably one of the biggest things I cherish, with being a part of the Liberty University Football program. Ed Gomes is a huge inspiration to my life, and the one- on-one, man-to-man accountability has taught me how to live my life correct, as a man. It has been something that I will have for the rest of my life

_Richard Wright All-American Long Snapper

Meeting with Ed Gomes one on one has provided an opportunity for accountability and a time of spiritual development and growth. Every Tuesday I look forward to hearing the advice of someone wiser than me, as well as being able to share my own stories with him. His Leaving a Legacy discipleship has really resounded in me; it is something I want and need to hear as a young man and an athlete. The material has such a broad spectrum, from how to choose the right person to date, to how to be a leader to my teammates; it is extremely beneficial to get a spiritual foundation on all of these subjects. Meeting with Ed has been an awesome experience that I have thoroughly enjoyed; he is an awesome mentor and friend

_Andrew Cordasco Tight End

My weekly meetings have offered a time of refreshment through discussing of the Word of God. They have been a great time of accountability as well as encouragement. Weekly meetings with Ed Gomes are comfortable and casual; making it easy to share what has been going on in our lives with each other

_Eric Fath Linebacker

The weekly meetings with Ed Gomes have been very beneficial not only in learning about God, but also using you as an accountability partner in my walk with Christ. Going through a different lesson each week really enhanced my knowledge and wisdom on different subjects

_Garrett Long Tight End

My one-on-one time with Ed Gomes was one of the best experiences of my life and allowed me to grow spiritually in Christ to really tune into my relationship with Jesus Christ we shared many laughs and many times that were serious and we learned a lot of life lessons together and how to be a better Christian and how to be a better man of God this time with him made a huge difference in my life and I am so thankful that I got to experience what I got to experience in his office! These are times I'll never forget and I highly recommend it to any player on Liberties football team

_Dexter Robbins Linebacker

My weekly meeting with Coach Gomes was a form of accountability. We were able to talk about real life problems and work on developing habits that help me to become a better man. Also, I learn how to take what I am learning through collegiate football and apply that to life so I can be a leader that models Christ in all stages of life

_Trey Turner Punter

My time with Ed Gomes was essential to my spiritual growth at Liberty. Ed was a true spiritual father to me, coming from a home where faith was not a priority; he taught me how to become a man of God. Our meetings built character, love, and respect. It didn't matter the situation, Coach was always there to uplift me, guide me, and support me. There were lots of laughs, lots of jokes, and some tears. But through thick and thin, I could, and still can, count on coach to be there for me as my spiritual coach! So I am extremely grateful for my time with Ed Gomes

_Zack Schreiber Linebacker

The one on one time with Ed Gomes has helped guide, mentor, and encourage me to be a better man on and off of the field. He shows a genuine love for the Lord and everyone he comes in contact with. I have great respect and love for Ed Gomes. He has poured encouragement and Biblical wisdom into my relationship with the Lord and my wife. I am thankful to have had Ed Gomes as a mentor

_Aaron Waller Defensive Lineman

The one on one time meant a lot to me. Especially, during my first semester at Liberty University. That was a time where I was lost, I was not sure who I was, why I was at Liberty and whether or not I wanted to stay. It was during the one on one time with Gomes that I received constant confirmation that I was a child of God and that I was placed at Liberty University with purpose and that God's plans were great for me. Gomes spoke truth and life into my life and taught me how to be a man of God. Through his words, I was given confidence in what Christ was doing. Through his actions, I learned how to be a servant, especially when no one was watching

_Miles Hunter Defensive Back

Every week, I would meet with Ed Gomes. I can still remember the "Hammer and Chisel Principle" and the many lessons I learned through our time. Gomes would impart wisdom to me through one-on-one discipleship. It was during his time that I was challenged most to take small steps of obedience to honor the Lord. I am so thankful that the Lord put Ed and his discipleship tool in my life to help guide me through college athletics

_Javen Shashaty Quarterback: Luke 2:52 Award recipient and Rock Royer / Mac Rivera Award

Introduction Material According to Alphabetical Order

- [ ] A. How to Effectively Use the Life Changing Principles
- [ ] B. How to Get the Most from Studying the Life Changing Principles
- [ ] C. How to Use the Topic, Verse, Ice Breaker Question, Principles, Quote, and Key Question when Teaching the Life Changing Principles
- [ ] D. How to Use the One on One Format for Teaching the Life Changing Principles
- [ ] E. How to Use the Team Format for Teaching the Life Changing Principles
- [ ] F. How to Utilize the Purpose, Goal, and Expectation of the Life Changing Principles
- [ ] G. How to Put into Action a Spiritual Game Plan to Impact an Entire Team through the Life Changing Principles

Discipleship lessons According to Alphabetical Order

☐ 21. How to Act Properly On a Date

☐ 22. How to Apply God's Word

☐ 23. How to Apply the Hammer and Chisel Principle

☐ 24. How to Avoid Making Harmful Decisions

☐ 25. How to Avoid Spiritual Complacency

☐ 26. How to be Salt and Light to My Teammates

☐ 27. How to Be a Leader On and Off the Field

☐ 28. How to Be a Spiritual Leader

☐ 29. How to Be an Example to Teammates

☐ 30. How to Be Available for God to Use me to Impact Teammates

☐ 31. How to Be Socially Accepted Without Compromising

☐ 32. How to Change the Habit of Lying or Cheating

☐ 33. How to Choose the Right Person to Date

☐ 34. How to Coach Myself

☐ 35. How to Deal with Conflict

☐ 36. How to Deal with Sexual Temptation

- [ ] 37. How to Demonstrate Leadership
- [ ] 38. How to Determine a Possible Vocation in Life
- [ ] 39. How to Develop and Identify Spiritual Leaders
- [ ] 40. How to Develop a Biblical Philosophy of Ministry
- [ ] 41. How to Develop a Daily Game Plan in Life
- [ ] 42. How to Develop an Attitude of Gratitude
- [ ] 43. How to Develop First-Class Dating Standards
- [ ] 44. How to Develop Champions for Christ
- [ ] 45. How to Develop Good Character for Everyday Life
- [ ] 46. How to Develop Winnings Habits that Contribute to Success
- [ ] 47. How to Develop My Relationship with God
- [ ] 48. How to Develop Safeguards for Using Social Media
- [ ] 49. How to Discern the Will of God
- [ ] 50. How to Disciple Another Teammate
- [ ] 51. How to Discover Characteristics of a Disciple-Maker
- [ ] 52. How to Display Character Through My Actions
- [ ] 53. How to Earn the Right to be Heard
- [ ] 54. How to Eliminate Excuses

☐ 55. How to Encourage Teammates

☐ 56. How to End a Relationship Correctly

☐ 57. How to Find a Good Church at Home and at School

☐ 58. How to Gain Valuable Insight from Others

☐ 59. How to Get Involved in a Ministry

☐ 60. How to Get the Most Out of My College Experience

☐ 61. How to Get the Most Out of My Elementary, Jr. and Sr. High School Experience

☐ 62. How to Have Life Changing Time in God's Word Everyday

☐ 63. How to Help a New Believer Grow Spiritually

☐ 64. How to Identify Positive Qualities of a Role Model

☐ 65. How to Incorporate the Essentials for Spiritual Growth

☐ 66. How to Keep a Good Conscience

☐ 67. How to Know How We should Teach Character

☐ 68. How to Know I am a Christian

☐ 69. How to Know If My Walk is Matching My Talk

☐ 70. How to Know the Difference Between Judging and Discernment

- ☐ 71. How to Know the Difference Between Root and Surface Problems
- ☐ 72. How to Know What Character Is
- ☐ 73. How to Know What We Should Do with God's Word
- ☐ 74. How to Know When We Should Teach Character
- ☐ 75. How to Know Where We Should Teach Character
- ☐ 76. How to Know Why We Should Teach Character
- ☐ 77. How to Live Out the Elementary, Jr. and Sr. High School and Athletic Team Mission
- ☐ 78. How to Live Out the University and Team Mission
- ☐ 79. How to Maintain Purity in a Relationship with the Opposite Sex
- ☐ 80. How to Make My Position My Primary Ministry
- ☐ 81. How to Memorize God's Word
- ☐ 82. How to Mentor Teammates
- ☐ 83. How to Minister to Teammates in the High-Interest Group
- ☐ How to Minister to Teammates in the No-Interest Group
- ☐ 85. How to Minister to Teammates in the Some-Interest Group
- ☐ 86. How to Offer Constructive Criticism to a Teammate

- [ ] 87. How to Overcome Past Failure
- [ ] 88. How to Pass on to Others What I am Learning
- [ ] 89. How to Pray for Teammates
- [ ] 90. How to Prepare for Life After College
- [ ] 91. How to Prepare to Be a Godly Husband
- [ ] 92. How to Prepare to Be a Godly Man
- [ ] 93. How to Prepare to Be a Godly Wife
- [ ] 94. How to Prepare to Be a Godly Women
- [ ] 95. How to Process Life Situations Properly
- [ ] 96. How to Properly Prepare for Engagement
- [ ] 97. How to Properly Prepare for Marriage
- [ ] 98. How to Read the Gauges of Life Correctly
- [ ] 99. How to Read My Spiritual Keys
- [ ] 100. How to Rebuild Trust After it Has Been Broken
- [ ] 101. How to Recognize Healthy Characteristics of a Disciple
- [ ] 102. How to Recognize the Different Stages of Relationships
- [ ] 103. How to Reproduce Spiritual Leaders
- [ ] 104. How to Respond to Constructive Criticism

☐ 105. How to Respond to People and Situations with Character

☐ 106. How to Respond to Temptation

☐ 107. How to Select an Accountability Partner

☐ 108. How to Share My Testimony and Present the Gospel

☐ 109. How to Show Leadership in All Four Areas of Whole Person Development

☐ 110. How to Start Your Day off Well

☐ 111. How to Stay Away From Pornography

☐ 112. How to Study God's Word

☐ 133. How to Talk with Someone About Personal Issues

☐ 114. How to Think Correctly About God, Self and Others

☐ 115. How to Turn Insecurities into Securities

☐ 116. How to Turn Problems into Opportunities

☐ 117. How to Understand the Process of Changing Negative Behavior

☐ 118. How to Understand the Realities of College Life as a Student-Athlete

☐ 119. How to Understand Who I am in Christ

☐ 120. How to Understand the Whole Person Development Model

- [ ] 121. How to Understand Why God Uses Circumstances in Our Lives

- [ ] 122. How to Understand the Yearly Cycle of a Champion Athlete

- [ ] 123. How to Use Biblical Principles When Dealing with Questionable Matters

- [ ] 124. How to Visualize My Role as the Spiritual Leader in My Position Group

- [ ] 125. How to Walk in the Spirit While Participating In a Sport

M = My turn

Y = Your turn

D =Discussion

Resources for Character Development

Character Websites:
Character Education Curriculum
www.characterandleadership.com
Character That Counts
www.charcterthatcounts.org
Habitudes
insight@growingleaders.com

Books on Character:

Character Matters By: Thomas Lickona
Character Counts By: Rod Handley
Character Counts By: J. C. Watts Jr.
Coaching for Character By: Dan Gerdes
Integrity By: Regal Books
Character Matters By: Mark Rutland
Patterns By: Mel Lawrenz
Revolution of Character By: Dallas Willard
Sport and Character By: Craig Clifford
Coach Wooden's
Pyramid of Success Playbook
By: John Wooden
Teaching Character Through Sport
By: Bruce Eamon Brown

Made in the USA
Columbia, SC
09 June 2019